SHELTERING STRANGERS
Critical Memoirs from Hosting Ukrainian Refugees

Daniel Briggs

P

First published in Great Britain in 2025 by

Policy Press, an imprint of
Bristol University Press
University of Bristol
1–9 Old Park Hill
Bristol
BS2 8BB
UK
t: +44 (0)117 374 6645
e: bup-info@bristol.ac.uk

Details of international sales and distribution partners are available at policy.bristoluniversitypress.co.uk

© Bristol University Press 2025

British Library Cataloguing in Publication Data
A catalogue record for this book is available from the British Library

ISBN 978-1-4473-7361-2 hardcover
ISBN 978-1-4473-7362-9 paperback
ISBN 978-1-4473-7364-3 ePub
ISBN 978-1-4473-7363-6 ePdf

The right of Daniel Briggs to be identified as author of this work has been asserted by him in accordance with the Copyright, Designs and Patents Act 1988.

All rights reserved: no part of this publication may be reproduced, stored in a retrieval system, or transmitted in any form or by any means, electronic, mechanical, photocopying, recording, or otherwise without the prior permission of Bristol University Press.

Every reasonable effort has been made to obtain permission to reproduce copyrighted material. If, however, anyone knows of an oversight, please contact the publisher.

The statements and opinions contained within this publication are solely those of the author and not of the University of Bristol or Bristol University Press. The University of Bristol and Bristol University Press disclaim responsibility for any injury to persons or property resulting from any material published in this publication.

Bristol University Press and Policy Press work to counter discrimination on grounds of gender, race, disability, age and sexuality.

Cover design: Liam Roberts Design
Front cover image: Unsplash/Tina Hartung

This book is dedicated to Oksana, her family and all the Ukrainians displaced or otherwise affected by a conflict that changed – and continues to change – their lives forever.

Contents

List of figures		vi
Acknowledgements		vii
1	The end at the beginning	1
2	Escaping the 'occupiers'	22
3	'We are not refugees! We are occupiers!'	40
4	Work, study and cultural integration	53
5	Strained relations and trending 'solidarity'	75
6	Pastures new and war sirens old	95
7	In search of *Slava Ukraïni*	115
References		136
Index		145

List of figures

1.1	Map of Madrid in relation to Brunete	2
2.1	Map of Madrid in relation to Brunete, Boadilla, Villaviciosa and Pozuelo	33
2.2	Initial arrivals (February/early March 2022)	35
3.1	Typical *Borshch* dish	44
3.2	Further arrivals (mid-to-late March 2022)	51
4.1	Maksym playing war games	56
4.2	Nadia and Milana walking together, with arms around each other's shoulders	69
5.1	Reshuffles (May 2022)	77
6.1	Autumn change (September 2022)	105
6.2	Nastia and Masha delivering a class	107
7.1	Christmas exodus (December 2022/January 2023)	121

Acknowledgements

I'm indebted to many people who have been involved in this unexpected project, notwithstanding all the Ukrainians who I came to know in my hometown of Brunete. To Oksana, Maksym, Nastia and Masha, I will make it to Ukraine one day. Valentin and Natasha, thank you for elucidating your early experiences in Spain and educating me around Ukrainian culture. The eccentric company of Valentyna and Anya was always lively and it was a pleasure to look after and play with their wonderful children, Ighor, Milana and the cheeky Yesenia. Aside from the geopolitical pressures, I wouldn't have met any of these people were it not for Malou, a friend of a friend whom I met only once in Barcelona. It was Malou who first passed me the hosting website through that friend during the first few weeks of the Russian/Ukrainian conflict, thus spurring everything that you read hereafter. I'm grateful to all my neighbours in Brunete who, in their own way, tried to do good things for the Ukrainians – even if it didn't quite turn out how they expected it. I am deeply indebted to my now lifelong friends Enrique and Belén who met with me and helped me clarify certain things at the point when many of the townsfolk were ostracising the Ukrainians and essentially asking them to leave their households.

My haphazard career now finds me working at Northumbria University where I am truly blessed to be working alongside my mentor and friend, Simon Winlow, and among some of most promising talent coming through the ranks in critical criminology such as Tom Raymen, Justin Kotzé, Nick Gibbs, Clare Wiper, Alex Hall, Georgios Antonopoulous and Mark Bushell. These people are a constant source of inspiration and also a good laugh. Outside this immediate environ, I am grateful for the collegiality of Gavin Oxburgh, Mike Rowe and Pam Davies, who, together with one of the largest criminology departments in the country, keep me sane and smiling between the mindless administrative tasks the university imposes on us. Notwithstanding, the great Steve Hall who also continues to be a source of inspiration and guidance and the good friendships I have with Luke Telford, Anthony Lloyd, Anthony Ellis, Craig Kelly, Stuart Taylor, Adam Lynes, James Treadwell and Tammy Ayres. Thank you to all the team at Bristol University Press and Policy Press, in particular Emily Ross for seeing the merit in the research and to Anna Richardson for her patience and direction during the publishing process. Last but not least, thank you to Lucy – ever a source for my creativity and ability to take on new challenges.

1

The end at the beginning

We sit outside on a sunny evening in the same café where we held the first host meetings. Eighteen months have passed since Russia invaded Ukraine in February 2022 and the same amount of time has passed since the town received numerous Ukrainian refugees. Sitting full in his chair to my left is Valentin; a large Ukrainian man in his mid-50s. Perched to my right is his wife, Natasha, also Ukrainian in her mid-40s. Both are from Kharkiv, a sizeable city in the northeast of the country only 30 kilometres from the Russian border. Perhaps unsurprisingly because of their age, they have memories of Ukraine when it pertained to the governance of the Soviet Union. In particular, Valentin recalls how 'the whole place was quite peaceful in the 1970s and 1980s. All we knew was limited, we went to work locally, we went home, we had little money, life was simple but we didn't dream because there was nothing to dream about'. While Valentin was born in Kharkiv, he had spent some time in Russia with his parents and was obliged to do military service during the 1980s before returning to Ukrainian territory after its independence from the Soviet Union in 1991. He laughs and his large structure makes the seat shudder when he says 'when I got my first passport, they said do you want Ukrainian or Russian. It wasn't difficult to choose! I am Ukrainian, I was born in Ukraine', before revealing that in doing so he was breaking historical and military ties with his Russian ancestry. 'My grandfather who fought in the Second World War for Russia would have been disappointed' he says jokingly as Natasha smiles. Natasha is ten years younger than Valentin so has fewer memories of the Soviet period:

> Until 17, I didn't even leave my town. I had my life in my town. When I was young, I thought my life would be in Kharkiv, work in the town, go to church in the town, marry someone in the town. We didn't have much money, my parents worked the land, farming, cultivating food. This was our life. (Natasha)

Valentin and Natasha describe a communist reality far from the neoliberalisation that was to occur in the aftermath of the fall of the Soviet Union. But things changed for Valentin and Natasha as they have lived in my hometown, Brunete – 27 kilometres from Spain's capital Madrid – for 20 years now (Figure 1.1). They arrived in Spain during the boom

Figure 1.1: Map of Madrid in relation to Brunete

Source: Map data © 2024 Google

immigration period at the turn of the 21st century, having moved from Ukraine after losing faith in a political and economic future. Over the course of this book, I will examine what this future was looking like for them when they decided to move but it is first important to note what they recount now: that, when they came, obtaining ID papers was very difficult, work opportunities were limited and there were huge bureaucratic challenges. It took many years for them to get settled in Spain. While Valentin continues to work in construction on the other side of the Madrid, Natasha has two jobs; one in the morning for a cleaning company and another in the afternoon at a local school as a classroom assistant. Together they earn a wage that permits them to 'just about get by' but that's about it. They manage to cover all the bills and will receive an ever-shrinking state pension but likely won't own their house mainly because they have been confined to the same sort of jobs in the same kinds of low-wage, precarious sectors since they arrived. The second important thing to note is, therefore, that their 'investment in a new social system' and 'years worked' haven't equated to a more secure future in Spain, which says something about the Western neoliberalisation of labour markets.[1]

Until February 2022, life had been quite peaceful for Valentin and Natasha but all that was to change when they would feature quite centrally in the arrival and support of numerous Ukrainian families to Brunete in the fallout of Russia's invasion of Ukraine. Unbeknown to them, they were to be key figures in the temporary housing and attempted cultural integration of these families along with other local Spanish families, including myself. We were to suddenly find ourselves caught up in the consequences of colossal historical and geopolitical processes, and for one reason or another, were either called into action or even called ourselves into action, to support a newly arrived, vulnerable immigrant group.

And this book is about what happened to these newly arrived Ukrainians in this small Spanish enclave that decided to open its doors in support of the cause of Europe's newest refugee group. It seeks to chart how and why the Ukrainians came to choose Brunete, how they settled and adapted to the expectations to work and start a new life. As I essentially documented what was happening as the Ukrainians arrived and settled, the book is rich in ethnographic detail and bolstered by contextual and theoretical material where required. Because I was one of those who hosted some of the families and witnessed first-hand their struggles, the text is probably first and foremost a chronological memoir if you like, mixed with my own thoughts and interactions with the Ukrainians alongside. However, because I am also a social researcher, the text is accompanied by a critical sociological analysis of the events: one which seeks to frame the subjective feelings and experiences of the Ukrainians against the new, unfamiliar and immediate socio-cultural environ of the Spanish host families as well as the wider global geopolitical arena.

So, on this day – 18 months after the invasion – I meet with Valentin and Natasha to reflect on all this. We sit and order drinks at the same table we had met previously when this all started; in the background there is a healthy babble of after-work chatter which mixes with the long sighs they make after I ask them about the experience of hosting Ukrainian refugees in hindsight:

Valentin:	Hmmm, [raises his eyebrows, sighs again as if he doesn't know where to start] it's an interesting question.
Natasha:	We have thought about it a lot [as her eyes look to the sky]. When you leave suddenly, you still leave with your home country in mind.
Valentin:	There is an internal conflict, two different cultures, opposite in some ways [the Spanish and Ukrainian]. It is a good thing to offer to help but no one here in Brunete or even in Spain was really prepared. No one really talked properly to the Ukrainian families about how they felt, what they wanted, what their hopes were. This didn't happen at all. It was bad communication. The Spanish tend to talk a lot but not really communicate how they are feeling about things, that's my experience of living here for 20 years.
Natasha:	We spoke about things directly with our Ukrainian family [whom they hosted]. You can do this, you can't do this, you have to contribute for this. But maybe it's because we understand the culture, the people and how they think.

	Most Ukrainians who came here thought they would just be given things. The problem was the Spanish felt sorry for them, treated them like they were poor and destitute, like they had nothing or could do nothing, like they needed their hand held and felt they had to do everything for them. The main problem was the Ukrainians didn't want that. The other problem is that the Spanish plan everything like Christmas, holidays, etc. Ukrainians don't: they just wait and see what happens tomorrow. It is more of a day-to-day thinking. People my age, 40 and upwards, they don't plan, they wait to be told, wait for things to be done for them.
Valentin:	It is a mentality.
Natasha:	In reality, only a few Spanish families adapted and managed it well: as in, they helped until the Ukrainians decided to do what they wanted. Most other [Spanish host families] just kicked the Ukrainians out … they just got tired of it, tired of them, they [the Spanish] put so much time and energy into it and felt it wasn't reciprocated in a way which they recognised as being appreciated.

This brief conversation gives you a small insight into the complexities of the brisk and unexpected arrival of 16 Ukrainian families to Brunete, my hometown, and the seven chapters that make up this book critically address what happened next. This introductory chapter merely sets the scene to the experiences of both Spanish host families and arriving Ukrainians by briefly looking at Russia and Ukraine, and the general global geopolitical spectrum before making a few statements about how this unexpected study came about. Chapter 2 focuses on the Russian invasion, drawing on testimonies from some of these families as they left Ukraine, where they went, how they felt and what led to them to find themselves in my hometown. In Chapter 3, the story of how the Ukrainians settled with their respective Spanish host families is presented and attention is given to the first few weeks of their new life in Spain. Chapter 4 marks a consideration of cultural integration, attempts to get work as well as early experiences in the exploitative labour market augmented by an increasing collective solidarity around the Ukrainians and their 'cause'.

Chapter 5 – much like this short exchange between Valentin and Natasha denotes – documents how this 'solidarity' starts to disintegrate. With the backdrop of the increasing cost of living (which, in part, the Spanish attribute to the Russia–Ukraine war) and mismatched cultural expectancies and idiosyncrasies, increased tension is felt between the Ukrainians and Spanish and this marks the rapid collapse of collective efforts to support them. Chapter 6 marks the widespread departure of most Ukrainian families from my hometown, in the main returning to Ukraine because of increased friction between guest and host, and because they felt guilty for leaving in the first place. Chapter 7, the epilogue, offers a conclusion alongside the current predicaments of all the protagonists and their ambitions for the future. Along the way, in every chapter and through every word, I hope to dissect the wider forces at play which determine what happens to the Ukrainians and their experiences as well as the attitudes and actions of the Spanish host families. For now, however, we need a little more context.

Russia and Ukraine: a brief history

Ukraine is now currently, once again, disputed territory but this is nothing new. Throughout history, its land and resources have been the subject for conflict and war involving the Mongol Empire, the Crown Kingdom of Poland and the Grand Duchy of Lithuania to name a few. During the industrial revolution, Ukraine was also contested by both Sweden and Russia. Its lands have also been shared somewhat. At the end of the 18th century, for example, vast proportions of Ukraine were governed by the Russian empire and Habsburg Austria. It wasn't until the 19th century, however, that ideologies around Ukrainian nationalism evolved. With the dissolution of the Habsburg monarchy as a consequence of the First World War, Russian revolutions ensued, and the subsequent Soviet–Ukrainian war then followed between 1917 and 1921. As a result of victory, led by the Russian Bolshevik Red Army who defeated Kyiv's national government in the early 1920s, the Ukrainian Soviet Socialist Republic was established, which was essentially one of the founding republics of the Soviet Union.

Soviet policy during the 1920s permitted Ukrainian language and culture to thrive throughout the country, its administration and in schools. However, during the 1930s, the policy shifted towards 'Russification' as Ukrainian independence initiatives emerged. This 'Russification' involved the introduction of new policies to retain Soviet ideology in line with expanding ambition to industrialise and decrease agricultural workforces. But these changes were to dramatically and fatally affect the main grain-producing areas of Soviet territory, in particular Ukraine, and the result was a widespread famine in the early 1930s. The subsequent *Holodomor*, meaning 'death by hunger' in Ukrainian, killed between six and nine million people across the Soviet Union, 5–6 million of which were estimated to be Ukrainian. Scholars seem to agree that the cause of the famine was directly related to these policies,[2] although others suggests that Joseph Stalin deliberately engaged the strategies to crush Ukrainian independence interests and cement allegiance to the Soviet Union.[3] There are also those, such as Andrea Graziosi, who suggests that the famine was an unintentional byproduct of the policies and that once it became embedded in the country's main agricultural areas, only then was it weaponised against the Ukrainians in order for any resistance to be quashed.[4] One of the most symbolic representations of this, Graziosi argues, was the transfer of Crimea from the Russian Communist Party to the Ukrainian Communist Party in 1954.

In the post Stalin-period of the mid-1950s, Nikita Khrushchev succeeded as the head of the Communist Party of the Soviet Union and initiated a revival of Ukraine. Resistance against Russia throughout third quarter of the 20th century continued as Ukrainians pressed for nationalisation but opposition was generally quickly quashed by the Soviet structure. Even when nationalisation was eventually achieved in 1991 – with the fall of the Soviet Union – most of Ukraine's early presidents maintained close ties with Russia (see also Chapter 2).[5] Today, socially and culturally speaking, research indicates that Ukrainians are not too dissimilar to Russians since many Ukrainians speak both languages and their histories and cultural practices are deeply intertwined with each other.[6] Yet Ukraine is now, as Jones states, 'a multi-ethnic, multi-religious and multi-lingual country with little historical experience of independent statehood'.[7] Russia, however, has continued along an autocratic pathway while, since its independence, Ukraine has embraced Western values of democratisation, privatisation and a market economy model, all of which were duly recognised by Valentin and Natasha. Recalling the early days of the independence, things like job 'opportunities' and 'consumer goods' started to enter Ukrainian social life, which started to alter the national psyche:

Valentin: In the 1990s, people started to change and want new things, goods, better life when the countries separated. You started to see it in work opportunities and the chance to earn more money.

Natasha: When it happened [the separation from the Soviet Union] it felt like we had been lied to for a lifetime. When I moved to Kyiv, it opened my eyes. There was hot water, the electricity didn't go off, heating, bigger shops, more variety. I started working with Americans and it opened my mind. This was when I started to change.

As a new state, however, power and control swiftly came under the increasing influence of oligarchs who emerged in Ukraine as the politically connected *nouveau riche* whose power was assembled through scavenging the 'remnants of the Soviet economy' via the corrupt yet democratically elected government of Ukraine in its transition to a market economy.[8] In the wake of its democratic infancy the power grab meant that Ukraine slumped into economic turmoil through corruption, fund mismanagement and debt, much of which was later to be exacerbated by the 2008 financial crisis.

Despite this, and even in the same year for example, the combined wealth of Ukraine's 50 richest oligarchs was equal to 85 per cent of Ukraine's gross domestic product.[9] Still the oligarchs maintained political and economic control, which meant that even in the wake of a new democracy, very little changed in Ukraine. In fact, almost all of Ukraine's presidents from the early 1990s to 2019 – Leonid Kravchuk, Leonid Kuchma, Viktor Yushchenko, Viktor Yanukovych and even the stand-in Oleksandr Turchynov – were involved in high-profile corruption, fraud, censorship, cronyism, repression of protest, abuse of power, theft, vote rigging, and strange disappearances of opposition or public resistance figures.

While the oligarchical pillaging and plundering of the Ukrainian economy thrust many of its citizens into poverty, one of the most significant triggers of discontent was the disappearance and murder of the opposition journalist, Georgiy Gongadze, at the hand of Ukraine's second president, Leonid Kuchma, in 2000. Gongadze had openly questioned Kuchma's governmental mismanagement in public interviews about his involvement in state-level corruption and personal siphoning of public money. He complemented these recorded open critiques with the launch of a socio-political publication, *Ukrainska Pravda*, meaning 'Ukrainian Truth'. The subsequent 'Cassette Scandal' revealed how Kuchma was secretly recorded speaking to other officials about how to dispose of Gongadze. In September 2000, Gongadze was kidnapped, killed and decapitated and wasn't found until a few months later in a nearby forest. The killing created a mass civic uprising culminating in the call for 'Ukraine Without Kuchma', which became an important precursor to the 2004/5 Orange Revolution: a popular protest movement which evolved because of the corruption and censorship in response to the fraudulent election of Viktor Yanukovych, Kuchma's handpicked successor (also see Chapter 2).

It was this election between Viktor Yanukovych, who was supported by Russia, and Viktor Yushchenko, a Western-oriented candidate, which created significant controversy and this was why 2004 marked the first significant point in the fateful division between Western-backed interests in Ukraine and Russian-backed interests. Yanukovych was the Russian-backed prime minister who controlled the traditional heavy industries of Donbas and Ukraine's economic links with Russia. His opponent, Yushchenko, was governor of Ukraine's central bank during the Western privatisation of the 1990s and campaigned on a promise to stop oligarchs and the plundering of the economy.[10] Even though Yushchenko was mysteriously poisoned before the election, he was able to recover. In the end, however, victory was declared in favour of Yanukovych. Subsequent investigations, however, found the election to have been fraudulent. Ukrainians took to the street wearing orange, which was Yushchenko's campaign colour. By December 2004, protests known as 'Euromaidan' were able to force a re-vote, resulting in a victory for Yushchenko. Within months, however, Yushchenko was accused of corruption and his supporters became disillusioned and abandoned his cause. It was this political and economic mismanagement, and subsequent social turmoil, which were to be the main reasons why Valentin and Natasha left their country and sought to start their lives again in Spain:

Valentin: I mean Ukrainian politics has always been corrupt but the first major scandal was with Kuchma who was behind the disappearance of Gongadze, the journalist. This was around 2000. Gongadze had disappeared, then his body was found without a head, then a witness in the murder case was killed I think. It was reported as suicide.

Natasha: I don't really get involved in politics, it doesn't interest me. I don't like it. When things really started to get bad when Yanukovych came into power, it made me feel sick, even if he was overturned. The country under the next president didn't change. Empty promises like all politicians.

As the 2010 election drew closer, Yanukovych started to win his voters back. After committing to work towards a relationship with the European Union (EU), Yanukovych shifted the political direction and began to reorient Ukraine towards Russia again. Yet Yanukovych was thought to be even more corrupt than his predecessors and installed family members to assist in running his business empire, which thrived off the Ukrainian economy.[11] This, combined with the controversial arrest of political opponent Yulia Tymoshenko, triggered widespread protests about perceived government corruption. Further protests erupted across the country, centring on Maidan Square in Kyiv and at least 130 people, primarily civilians, were killed. Meanwhile, Yanukovych fled to Russia, and the new Western-backed leadership started to pivot Ukraine, once again, towards the EU.

Even if it had been posing as a democratic nation under post-Soviet reform and privatisation, Ukraine couldn't shake the cancerous influence of the oligarchs and the corrupt political elite and business owners. It did, however, start to increase trade with Europe, continued to welcome the idea of North Atlantic Treaty Organization (NATO) enlargement and obtained a visa-free regime with the countries of the EU. Indeed, speculation around its incorporation into the EU as well as NATO was part of a wider movement which had gathered momentum while European state membership had gradually been moving east. In March 2004, Bulgaria, Estonia, Latvia, Lithuania, Romania, Slovakia and Slovenia, for example, all joined NATO. Yet Ukraine has historically been considered to be Russia's 'breadbasket', rich in natural energy supplies and food produce but when other nations were perceived to have 'started to eat from the basket', it was said that this provoked Russia.[12] Explicit warning signs of what could happen if Ukraine were to fully commit to such endeavours were exposed with the Russian invasion of Georgia, undertaken in the main to counter negotiations for its NATO membership. Richard Sakwa said at the time how:

> In the end, NATO's existence became justified by the need to manage the security threats provoked by its enlargement. The former Warsaw Pact and Baltic states joined NATO to enhance their security, but the very act of doing so created a security dilemma for Russia that undermined the security of all.[13]

Indeed, one Russian news media reported that, in conversation with President Bush, Putin very transparently hinted that if Ukraine was accepted into NATO, it would cease to exist. Indeed:

> The West's final tool for peeling Kyiv away from Moscow has been its efforts to spread Western values and promote democracy in Ukraine and other post-Soviet states, a plan that often entails funding pro-Western individuals and organizations. Victoria Nuland, the U.S. assistant secretary of state for European and Eurasian affairs, estimated in December 2013 that the United States had invested more than $5 billion since 1991 to help Ukraine achieve 'the future it deserves'.[14]

Much of this stoked Russian political concern for Ukraine's Western-backed drift towards NATO[15] and simultaneously reconfigured and re-energised geopolitical rivalry between the two, aptly reflected in the alternating power grabs from either pro-European or pro-Russian presidents:[16] a tendency difficult to counter since Ukraine has been – and still is – historically divided by a Ukrainian-speaking west and centre and a Russian-speaking south and east.[17] The most prominent example of this was when American-backed protests erupted in the lead up to the 2014 presidential elections as a result of Yanukovych rejecting a major economic deal he had been negotiating with the EU and instead accepting a US$15 billion Russian counter-offer. Other issues compounded his legitimacy, such as overt attempts to remove opposition members, press censorship, corruption and consolidating oligarchical cronyism.

In the political vacuum of his exile, the Crimea was annexed by Russia in part because Putin feared it could become a NATO naval base.[18] Widespread corruption, poverty and political neglect were already previously endemic in Crimea and its decaying industries and depressed communities exacerbated by free-market neoliberal policies were to form the social conditions that generated support and submission to Putin's occupation.[19] By the beginning of March 2014, Russian soldiers had occupied the whole area, taken over communications and state-led institutions, installed Russian currency, and shut down Ukrainian websites relating to government, news media and social media. Mearsheimer even warned at the time how:

> [T]his grand scheme went awry in Ukraine. The crisis there shows that realpolitik remains relevant – and states that ignore it do so at their own peril. U.S. and European leaders blundered in attempting to turn Ukraine into a Western stronghold on Russia's border. Now that the consequences have been laid bare, it would be an even greater mistake to continue this misbegotten policy.[20]

Despite this, still Ukraine persevered with the pursuit of a pro-European future. For example, a joint memorandum between the foreign ministers of Georgia, Moldova and Ukraine was drawn up to mark this direction. Known as the 'Association Trio', it was to commit to enhanced cooperation, coordination and dialogue between the three countries on issues of common interest relating to European integration, enhancing cooperation within the framework of the Eastern Partnership, and committing to the prospect of joining the EU. Unsurprisingly, in February 2022, Ukraine applied to join the EU and perhaps even more unsurprisingly, in the same month, Russia invaded Ukraine, seeing this as a direct threat to its national security interests and power standing. A more nuanced explanation of Russia's intentions then would thus frame the invasion in this context: NATO enlargement and expansion – which was seen as a threat to Russia – seemingly completed a wider strategy to integrate and align Ukraine to the West.[21] Indeed, since 1991, the United States has pumped at least US$5 billion into funding pro-democracy causes in Ukraine and this, among other things, acted as further provocation for Russia.[22] The United States even changed its own policy in 2017 to enable the sale of 'lethal weapons' to Ukraine, which it claimed were for 'defensive purposes'. This was perceived by Russia, however, as an 'offensive' manoeuvre.[23] Given that Russia has no main natural borders (such as oceans or rivers), its vast plains feed a sense that there is a constant threat from the West[24] and this, along with the possible NATO expansion, as well the introduction of new intermediate-range missile deployments in Ukraine, was thought to add to the collective rationale for the invasion of Ukraine.[25]

The wider geopolitical, structural, cultural and subjective contexts for this unexpected study

For these reasons, it's almost impossible to write this book without discussing the political, economic and social impact neoliberalism has had on the world since its rise in the late 20th century. Based on a political and economic philosophy which advocates free markets, deregulation and reduction in government spending, neoliberalism has been at the forefront of expanding economic growth and globalisation while also contributing to rising war and conflict, inequality, social disparities and environmental challenges. Because the rapid increase in free trade and open markets have facilitated the movement of goods, services and capital across borders, international trade and investment has soared, leaving few countries behind. Indeed, countries like Ukraine and Russia have both experienced significant economic, social and cultural transformations as a consequence of neoliberalism. This shift has also led to the growing influence of multinational corporations and financial institutions in shaping geopolitical relations, political parties, economic policies and priorities.

Perhaps most poignantly for this book, it is worth noting how the evolution of neoliberalism has gone hand in hand with increased investment in defence spending and the increased militarisation of international relations. The term 'military-industrial complex' (MIC) refers to the relationship between a country's military and the defence industry that supplies it with arms, among other military materials, as well as a marked influence over national policy, particularly regarding defence spending and foreign policy. Over the last decade, the MIC has had a profound impact on various conflicts and global military dynamics. Despite periods of economic austerity, many countries, particularly the United States, have at least maintained or increased their defence budgets, signifying how the MIC plays a major role in lobbying for high levels of military expenditure: often in the name of national security and the incumbent economic benefits.

The MIC has therefore facilitated extensive international arms sales, with major exporters like the United States, Russia and European countries supplying weapons to numerous nations, thus securing influence on foreign policy and political and economic alliances, as recipient countries become economically and militarily bound to their suppliers. Yet critics – such as John Mearsheimer – indicate that this international conglomerate of arms dealing prolongs conflicts and stimulates new rifts. The ongoing wars in Syria, Yemen and Afghanistan, for example, have been marked by sustained and continued arms supplies from global powers. The availability of advanced weaponry has therefore escalated violence and hindered peace processes because various factions receive continuous support from external military industries. Furthermore, the MIC drives the development of advanced military technologies, such as drones, cyber warfare tools and precision-guided munitions, and it is these technologies that have transformed modern warfare, making conflicts more asymmetrical. Some have even suggested that this drives the risk of reciprocal violent escalation and the speculation surrounding the possible use of nuclear weapons by Russia is a good example of this.[26] The neoliberal drive for profit therefore encompasses defence contractors' efforts to exert significant influence over political leaders and policy makers through lobbying and campaign contributions, which, in turn, result in policies that favour continued military investment and high defence spending. However, while such an endeavour may support millions of jobs and contribute to economic growth, the economic dependency on producing arms skews national priorities *towards sustaining military projects and engagements* such as the one we continue to see play out between Ukraine and Russia.

As described previously, the geopolitical tussle over Ukraine has been exacerbated by the adoption of market-oriented reforms, privatisation and deregulation in the 1990s aimed at transitioning it from a Soviet-style planned economy to a capitalist market economy. These reforms led to economic instability, increased inequality, and the concentration of wealth and power in the hands of its oligarchs. Public services and social safety nets weakened, exacerbating poverty and unemployment. In many countries, neoliberal reforms have been associated with the erosion of democratic institutions and processes because the prioritisation of economic efficiency over social and political considerations has been found to lead to policies that undermine democratic accountability and public participation. And Ukraine is no different in this respect. Such a concentration of wealth and power among a small elite – in this case the oligarchs – similarly raises concerns about the influence of money in politics and associated corruption. Indeed, the Council of Europe indicate that Ukraine is the most corrupt country in Europe after Russia.[27]

The ideological and geopolitical competition between the West/EU and Russia regarding their mutually exclusive or even antagonistic integration policies is now taking place within the shared territory of Ukraine.[28] While the Cold War presented the opportunity to redefine global relations, reduce military spending and instead reinvest resources in better future, much of this lost traction when a US and NATO collective sought to take advantage of collapse of the Soviet Union. In the words of Mitchell and Fazi, 'after the disintegration of the Soviet Union in the early 1990s and the United States rise to "hyperpower" status, the conditions emerged for the US to aggressively reassert its global hegemony'.[29] A revealing clue to this agenda is to be found in Thomas Friedman's *Manifesto for the Fast World*. Published by the *New York Times* in 1999, Friedman set out a case for the United States to embrace its role as the 'enforcer of the capitalist order' by writing that '[t]he hidden hand of the market will never work without the hidden fist … and the hidden fist that keeps the world safe for Silicon Valley technologies is called the US Army, Air Force and Marine Corps'.[30]

When Russia was subject to the resulting economic 'shock therapy' with the rapid privatisation of its national resources and state-owned industries in the post-Soviet era, the West – in particular the United States – continued to pursue NATO expansion, which now appears as one of the central dynamics contributing to the evolution and escalation of the present conflict.[31] Furthermore, as a way of rivalling US hegemony, in 2006, Russia started to meet informally with other emerging economies such as Brazil, India and China to enhance economic collaboration, reform global financial institutions and address common challenges. BRIC (Brazil, Russia, India, China) became a formality in 2009 after its first summit in Russia and, a year later, became BRICS when South Africa joined the initiative. Russia's vast natural resources, strategic location and political weight bolster BRICS's capacity to challenge Western dominance in global affairs as well as facilitates greater economic cooperation, trade and investment among member nations, contributing to a multipolar world order which has certainly threatened US global hegemony and thus provided further impetus for Western-backed support in Ukraine over the last 15 years.[32] The now waged 'proxy war' has therefore arisen as a consequence of Western, in particular, American geopolitical power interests affecting the long-established West–Russia relationship. These indicators are said to represent a more unstable international system, characterised by:

1. *The return of inequality*: relating to the increasing frequency of financial crisis and economic uncertainty which is growing precarity and poverty.
2. *The return of mass flight*: ongoing and mounting refugee crises from the Global South and far Eastern countries, stimulated by increasingly unstable political regimes, such as Libya, Syria, Yemen, and so on.
3. *The return of barbarism*: associated with international terrorism such as Islamic State and Al Qaeda and its related brutality of beheadings and executions.
4. *The return of the Cold War*: the state of conflict pursued via economic and political manoeuvres and/or proxy wars.

The current status quo underscores a global political economic context of fragile geopolitical relations, increased resource wars, unpredictable climate change, myriad economic inequality, increasing unemployment, growing precarious work and the rise of political dissatisfaction.[33] Exacerbated by the mismanagement of the COVID-19 pandemic,[34] such fracturing geopolitical relations only prize open wider the wounds of history as ominous strategies are exercised by the world's political heavyweight powers in the name of economic gain and political sovereignty. These are just some examples of what had come to be regarded as the morbid symptoms of an interregnum in Western nations.[35]

This focus on market efficiency and competition leads to wealth concentration among the few, leaving behind those who cannot compete. So, while powerful multinational corporations have flourished under neoliberalism by benefiting from lower trade barriers and deregulation, over the last 50 years, millions upon millions of people have become surplus to requirement as traditional industries and livelihoods have eroded, which has disproportionately impacted upon poor and marginalised communities. In Western countries, the dismantling of welfare states and labour protections has widened the gap between the rich and the poor, leaving a middle class – once the backbone of many economies – more precariously economically vulnerable as jobs have become more uncertain and wages have stagnated. Deregulation and the emphasis on flexibility have led to the proliferation of non-standard forms of employment, such as part-time, temporary, zero-hour contracts and 'gig economy' work. While these forms of employment can provide flexibility for some, they tend to lack the protections and benefits associated with traditional full-time jobs, leading to greater job insecurity and precariousness. To add to this, neoliberal policies have weakened the power of labour unions, which has reduced workers' bargaining power and limited their ability to campaign for better working conditions.

But because neoliberalism advocates for reduced government intervention in the economy, this often translates to cuts in public spending on social welfare, healthcare and public services. This has led to the privatisation of essential services such as healthcare, education and social security in the name of 'efficiency', which has, over time, made these services less accessible and affordable, particularly for the disadvantaged. Consequently, in many countries around the world, the reduction in public spending has strained social safety nets, leaving vulnerable people without adequate support. Moreover, the emphasis on 'individual responsibility' over 'collective welfare' has shifted the burden of social risks onto individuals. Importantly, as we will see in Chapters 3, 4 and 5, therefore, are that these socio-cultural and subjective ramifications mean that neoliberalism promotes an individualistic ethos where everything revolves around 'personal responsibility', 'entrepreneurship' and 'self-reliance', thus shaping the way people view success, failure and social responsibility. So, on one hand, this can foster and vitalise innovation and ambition, while, on the other, it can simultaneously result in a lack of empathy and collective solidarity, thus exacerbating social divisions and cultural expectations.

This is furthermore compromised by the influence of other features of neoliberal life. Living in a fast-moving, highly competitive, market-driven environment produces a claustrophobic sense of being. *Claustropolitanism*, according to Redhead, refers to this social, cultural or philosophical outlook characterised by a sense of confinement, restriction or limitation, often associated with urban living, tightly controlled environments or limiting lifestyles.[36] It reflects the feeling of being 'closed in' by the physical, social or psychological boundaries levied by modern life. This concept is often contrasted with *cosmopolitanism*, which embraces openness, diversity and a global outlook – one which Western political elites tend to tout these days and one which celebrates a 'everyone-can-get-on-well-with-everyone' mantra.[37] *Claustropolitanism* emphasises the constraints, pressures and challenges of navigating life in an increasingly interconnected but also pressurised and restrictive world. Borrowing from Virilio, Redhead sought to critique the failure of cosmopolitanism by positing that Western societies were instead veering towards a very different trajectory: instead, swathes of people, he claimed, were pining to escape the pathologies of the real world and retreat into a kind of defensive individualism buttressed by consumer markets. Such a vista confines authentic intersubjective exchanges – ones which encourage learning from others and make meaningful personal reflections possible – and instead approximates people towards a sense of apprehension and aversion in social situations.[38]

Impediments to the ability to connect and empathise with the social is exacerbated by the rate at which technology and the media guide human perception and identity. Such an acceleration of life – driven by technological advancements and the constant flow of information – fundamentally alters how individuals experience the world and themselves. This was the principal argument made by Virilio, who suggested that this rapid pace creates a sense of disorientation and fragmentation in subjectivity, where people feel increasingly detached from their physical environments and even from their own bodies. *Dromology* (the logic of speed), he claimed, explains how modern society's obsession with *speed* leads to a loss of depth in human experience, makes us impatient and reduces our capacity for reflection. This results in a more superficial, unstable sense of self, overwhelmed by the influence of media and technology, unable to grasp meaningful understandings of the world, how it works and people's circumstances.[39]

This subjective dead end is also complemented by a political torpor. Indeed, in their analysis of contemporary societies, Winlow and Hall argue that many people these days, including political leaders and the general public, increasingly ignore or deny the deep social problems caused by neoliberal capitalism, such as inequality, poverty and social fragmentation. Such disavowal, they say, results in a lack of meaningful political engagement and a failure to address systemic issues, leaving societies stuck in a state of apathy and inertia, much like that which Valentin and Natasha displayed in their condemnation of the Ukrainian political system.[40] Indeed, when we look at Ukraine's painful birth from the fallout of the Soviet Union, the same pattern emerges. New hope was presented in the form of the Ukrainian independence from Russia but powerful entrepreneurs and political elites were poised to plunder the new opportunities to capitalise on the formation of the new state.[41] Ukraine evolves with the same economic teething problems of wealth confinement, oligarchical control, stunted and staggered investment programmes, coupled with a spatially and ethnically divided electorate who, instead of experiencing progress and prosperity, economic reform and political stability, only got to watch on as their new country developed all the insalubrious trademarks of the former Soviet regime.

In the years since its break from the Soviet Union in 1991, Ukraine has experienced a deepening population loss due to negative birth rates and high migration dynamics – and Valentin and Natasha are testament to this. For example, although Ukraine had a population of 51.5 million after gaining independence, in 2019 its estimated population size was a mere 37 million.[42] Such international migration has gained prominence in this era of globalisation with the trend towards greater economic integration opening new cross-border opportunities for labour. Today, more people than ever live in a country other than the one in which they were born. According to the Population Division of the United Nations Department of Economic and Social Affairs, as of 1 July 2020 the global number of international migrants was estimated to be 281 million. While some move in search of better economic opportunities or to study, others do so to escape climate-related disasters, persecution and war. Valentin and Natasha are living examples of the former while their soon-to-be-arriving family members in Ukraine were to be surviving examples of the latter.

The annexation of Crimea in 2014 meant that the two main receivers of Ukrainians were Poland and Russia, largely due to liberal and flexible migration policies. The subsuming of the Crimea to Russian power prompted a major increase in the number of Ukrainians seeking employment in the EU member states and has since been enabled further by simplified procedures for entering the Schengen zone (a visa-free regime has been in place since 2017). While the latter doesn't entitle Ukrainians to take up work in these countries, it instead tends to facilitate travel and the possible further legalisation of their residence there. A socio-political context of increased population movement and diminishing economies – largely because of the aforementioned – converts a populace towards individualistic thinking and into entrepreneurial means of survival within a context of increased competition for work in host countries, and this was why Valentin and Natasha found their first few years in Spain challenging.

Researcher, activist, supporter?

It is the human consequences of these economic shifts, historical processes and strained geopolitical relations that I try to discuss in depth in this text: about how macro-processes of geopolitics instigate forced migration, and how people start again in another country, how they culturally assimilate and settle. I was fortunate to get a first-hand insight into this when I received a Ukrainian family in my home in March 2022, one month into the conflict.

I found myself in a situation unfamiliar to me where, on one hand, I was *helping* as well as *researching* the situation. I've done many ethnographic studies over the last 25 years, during which I have seen at varying points the gruesome depths of suffering in society. Sadly, while I have gone on to write and talk about them as much as possible, I've rarely seen social policy change let alone positive social change, which speaks volumes about the protracted determination of the neoliberal political economic model to continue to exhaust itself, even in the face of its own extinction.[43]

No institution or entity has been able to escape the effect of this system, which is why its influence has had a profound impact on universities and social study because it has corporatised academic life and expanded governance over critical social research. It has straight-jacketed us into conceiving that 'research' must involve the acquisition of money from 'reputable' funding bodies who determine political and social agendas as well as favour lacklustre methodologies and same-answer solutions. It has persuaded us that the answer to our potential influence over improving social life and all its injustices lies in the production of dry policy briefs and jargonised articles in only the 'highest impact factor journals', which few read outside academia. It beckons us to indulge and compete in accumulating citations as a means of measuring our 'excellence' and feed our intellectual vanity by throwing one-liners and selfies on social media to obtain 'likes'. In the end, the potential we have to report on and intervene in what is happening in the world is dramatically hindered by these bureaucratic distractions. So, another consideration to the way in which I have done this study is because the social sciences are currently not producing enough cutting-edge research which responds to 21st-century social realities.

It's also probably why I now actively help people involved in research studies. Social research shouldn't be such a one-sided process where we confine people to being labelled 'subjects'. I think we should demonstrate empathy, care and support for the people we study and help them where we can. When I was challenged on this issue at a recent conference, I said to the panel and the audience that too often in our social science works, the few that are still in the game of doing edgy fieldwork will generally be expected to access vulnerable people we call 'participants', persuade them to give up sensitive information about their lives, which we call 'data', and then leave – having fully benefited from that information – to convert it into unnecessarily long-worded and meaningful knowledge outputs. The purpose? To write these outputs as inaccessible journal articles which the vast majority of everyday people will never read yet thereafter foist them on our students for years as proof that we are intellectuals and worthy of the PhD for which we studied. As a sidebar, and if we are lucky, the right people in positions of responsibility might come across our research and read a page of it. But, generally, that's as far as it goes, and the words and publications get confined to history. This says much about our political, economic and social stasis.[44]

I believe there is no harm in actually making research a reciprocal exchange: *I will help you with what I can within my power if you can share with me your intimate experiences and feelings.* The people you read about in this book agreed to this and my pledge to them was that I would write about them in a way that retained their dignity and humanity; I would protect their identity so their vulnerability was not compromised and laid bare; and I would describe them as *people* rather than a *participant* or *statistic* and would find the precise words to describe how they came to experience, feel and think as they did. These are, I think, the ethical pledges we should make to people we study and really this is the direction we should be taking to reverse the conceptual and theoretical rot endemic to our discipline as a consequence of its submission to corporate influence.[45] For all these reasons, and for some years, I have abandoned seeking large-scale, standardised and mainstream funding calls, preferring instead self-funded studies that are free from bureaucracy and which can follow social issues 'as they happen'. Like almost all the studies I have undertaken, particularly over the last decade, there is no funding attached to this work.

The study you are about to read about was also done, by the most part, covertly – that is, without the knowledge of the 'participants'. With experience, though, I have found that researcher identity – though complexly bound up with issues of informed consent – immediately transforms how people interact and what they may choose or choose not to share. This changes the 'quality' of data and, because of that, potentially skews results and conclusions. There is something crudely pure about covert ethnographies, something which makes you more aware of how you exercise your research identity probably because you must apply an additional layer of reflexive awareness. You *not only have to be alert to the fact that you are unknown as a researcher* but also that *everything you do has the potential to reveal it.*

In the pages which await you and, at every opportunity, I have tried to use such covert approaches diligently: the sole purpose being to delicately and carefully build a holistic picture of the social reality under study without harming people or potentially perpetuating their situations. I have gained the full consent in hindsight from all the Ukrainians mentioned in this book. The Ukrainians that appear central in this text whom I came to know in my hometown, over time and at the right moment, were also made aware of my intentions as a researcher and my willingness to publish their stories and experiences. They continue to give me updates about their lives, send me photos and we still have good, solid and open relationships. I think this is because they still seek diverse platforms to talk about what has happened to them and what continues to happen in their country. All their names are anonymised for the purposes of the book and information which could otherwise result in their identification are also disguised – even if they consented them to be publicly known.

Regarding the Spanish host families, I introduced myself and my profession as a researcher from the outset but didn't declare that I was potentially gathering data from the host meetings, events and parties which I attended. There was a deliberate reason for this because, during this experience, I was having to balance two perspectives which hardened only as the hosting experience unfolded: the Ukrainians viewing hosts at times as 'unsympathetic to their cause' and 'inflexible' versus the Spanish viewing the Ukrainians as 'freeloaders' and often 'idle'. Naturally, the gradual tension which I come to explore in detail in the book demanded that, one by one, those Spanish host families involved were required to sit on one side of the fence. Essentially, I didn't want to fall either side and flank the Ukrainians or the Spanish host families because it would have interrupted my ability to document how each side was feeling. To do this, I had to maintain a sympathetic and empathetic viewpoint for each group's circumstances and views. With more specific reference to the Spanish host families, declaring my intentions to research and document at that time would have certainly limited potential information they confided in me about how they really felt. A good ethnographer *never necessarily declares where he/she stands*, only that *they he/she is standing if you like: the only side they appear to take is everyone's side* without 'anyone' knowing *they are necessarily in the business of siding*. In any case, and likely because of the diminished importance of the whole hosting experience and prominence of the war in the collective conscious, when I returned to speak to these families, I explained how I would like to write a book about the experience, at which point they gave their consent.

The aims of this book

The book is not only about the dilemmas generated from the 'hosting-a-refugee' experience, but it is also about wider concerns about the conjuncture of our present-day world. The out-of-control pursuit of power and profit, people movement, problems of modern-day cultural integration, the structural imbalances in the economy and labour market, the confused moral quandary of how and why 'help' to help fellow humans, are all bound to harmful paradigms produced by neoliberal capitalism. It is hoped that this book will allow people – you, the reader – to see this more clearly in slow motion. Moreover, the imminence of a war disrupts social life in so many unfathomable and unobvious ways, which is why the interrogation and analysis of these schisms is another objective of the text.

I have tried to stay true to everyone and present, in real terms, their experiences and scaffold them within the current cultural, political and economic contours of neoliberal capitalism. The structure of the book is straightforward, the style is refreshingly honest, and I would say it is unusually easy to read for an academic text. More than anything, I want people to understand *how* and *why* things have happened as they did and *how* and *why* people have behaved as they did. There is no easy way to receive unknown guests into your home and know what to do, as there is no blueprint for people to follow who leave their country because of forces outside their control and start again somewhere else. Still, the *ideological expectation* – reflecting neoliberalism's deep manifestation in human subjectivity – that people are responsible only for themselves is living and breathing in all of us:

> Katya and Karina [young Ukrainian women] didn't leave [Spain], they still work here. Karina is exemplary of how it should be done. She learned the language, writing her CV in Spanish as she was training to [become] a dentist. Now she has had two jobs in dentists, and she is earning reasonable money. The bosses are very happy with her. And I know Spanish people, lazy people, who say it's hard to find work. Well, you have to work hard to find it! (Valentin)

Notes

1. Map data ©2024 Google.
2. Lloyd (2018).
3. Kas'ianov (2010); Andriewsky (2015).
4. Graziosi (2004); Stark (2010); Mass (2013).
5. Graziosi (2004).
6. Matuszak (2012).
7. Jones (2022).
8. Onuch and Hale (2017).
9. Yurchenko (2017).
10. Taras (2008).
11. Benjamin and Davies (2022).
12. Benjamin and Davies (2022).
13. Sakwa (2014: 4).
14. Sakwa (2014: 4).
15. Mearsheimer (2014: 4).
16. Abelow (2022).
17. Nehring (2022).
18. Pop-Eleches and Robertson (2018).
19. Mearsheimer (2014).
20. Mearsheimer (2014: 2).
21. Gotz and Staun (2022).
22. Mearsheimer (2014).
23. Abelow (2022).
24. Mearsheimer (2022).
25. Sakwa (2021).
26. Abelow (2022).
27. Council of Europe (2018).
28. Council of Europe (2018).

29. Mitchell and Fazi (2017: 104).
30. Friedman (1999).
31. Benjamin and Davies (2022).
32. Mearsheimer (2022).
33. Parenti (2011); Briggs (2020); Telford (2022).
34. Briggs et al (2023).
35. Winlow et al (2015).
36. Redhead (2011).
37. Winlow and Hall (2022).
38. Redhead (2011); see also Virilio (2010).
39. Virilio (2010).
40. Winlow and Hall (2022).
41. Klein (2007).
42. Mulska et al (2020).
43. Mitchell and Fazi (2017); Winlow and Hall (2022).
44. Winlow et al (2015).
45. Hall (2012); Briggs (2022); Winlow and Hall (2022).

2

Escaping the 'occupiers'

The parakeets squawk and screech between Brunete's church bells sounding the arrival of 3pm on a Saturday afternoon. I am here to meet Katya and Karina who have been here in Spain for 18 months. Apart from Valentin and Natasha, they are the last two of the 60 Ukrainians I see regularly. As I come to learn, life has not been that easy for them in Spain: in fact, far more challenging than Valentin makes out. We sit and talk, and even though I've known them for 18 months, the vivid experiences of leaving Ukraine remain imprinted on their memories:

Karina: Many people dead, friends. I used to watch the news more but not like before. It is crazy if you follow it with everything you have.

Dan: I imagine that if you invest time in following it you would want to see progress or some sort of end.

Karina: The fireworks the other night [held because of local Madrid festivals] gave me a fright because it is light in the sky.

Katya: When I was working in the Jardineria [gardening], it made me fearful. Planes flying low, then helicopters sometimes and it felt like I was on alert again, it made me feel insecure. Because for a few weeks, it was all the noises I heard when I was in the basement. The shaking of the buildings and the ground when missiles and bombs landed … every one that came felt like it was going to hit us.

Karina: One of the hardest things for me was when I was in Kharkiv train station, trying to leave, both my parents were there and they were helping me to board the trains. Thousands of people, no room to move, I needed their shielding and protection. Suddenly, we hear planes above us. We hoped they were Ukrainian but they were Russian, and they were circulating around the station firing their guns randomly at the crowd. I won't forget this moment … [starts to well up with tears in her eyes]. It lives with me, it is even real now in my mind as I tell you.

Eighteen months previously, these experiences weren't something that Katya or Karina were able to talk about let alone reflect much on. In Katya's words, 'we weren't processing this sort of thing, we were on emergency autopilot, not thinking about what was happening … just focused on escaping how we could'. Katya left Ukraine with her mum, Olena, two younger brothers, Artem and Andrei, and her frail and elderly grandmother. They knew they would head to Spain because it was where Katya's aunt was living – Natasha, whom we met in Chapter 1. They had already been assured that they could stay in their humble three-bedroom flat and work out what to do. Karina's journey, on the other hand, was more precarious as she came by herself, travelling from Kharkiv to the Polish border on the train, hitching a lift in a car for a day over the border before taking a bus to Warsaw. She then took a plane to Madrid where she was reunited with her partner, Katya.

In our conversations, both Katya and Karina use 'Russians' interchangeably with 'occupiers'. The word 'occupation' refers to the action, state or period of occupying or being occupied by military force, but it also has connotations of a temporary condition. This is precisely how Katya and Karina as well as these families initially framed the Russian invasion – as a kind of short tenure which has slowly become a back-and-forth contest over Ukrainian territory. So, when they left Ukraine, naturally in fear and unknowing of what may happen, they framed their move as short term: something necessary but not permanent. This 'in-between' state produces two main subjective quandaries as it *hinders thinking about how to 'move on' in their new country* while, at the same time, *keeps them attached to Ukraine and the unfolding events*. This tension starts to reveal itself later in the book, but for now in this chapter, I want to look at some of the journeys the Ukrainians took and how and why they started to arrive in Brunete. Equally, I start to consider how and why some of the Spanish families got involved in hosting them.

From pre-occupation to preoccupation: barrage, bombing and bloodshed

The 2014 Russian occupation of Crimea, which followed a series of protests in the aftermath of the Euromaidan, prompted Russian troops to occupy key sites on the peninsula, wearing military uniforms with Russian insignias removed. The annexation created international outrage and was condemned by the United Nations and the European Union (EU). Yanukovych's disappearance was followed by the presidency of Petro Poroshenko in the same year, a pro-European president who then redirected Ukraine's course towards Europe by signing the European Union–Ukraine Association Agreement (see Chapter 1). The Ukrainian language, nationalism, inclusive capitalism, decommunisation and administrative decentralisation were also fundamental areas of his domestic policy as he became active in improving international relations with the United States and the EU. Notwithstanding, the subject of North Atlantic Treaty Organization (NATO) membership was revisited. While the demise of his presidency didn't sink to the same levels of disgrace as his predecessors', Poroshenko became involved in fraudulent activity and failed to prevent widespread corruption or tackle conflict in the Donbas – one of the main regions where persistent fighting had broken out in the wake of the 2014 Crimean annexation.

And it was to be Volodymyr Zelenskyy, a former comedian, who overwhelmingly defeated Poroshenko in the 2019 presidential election with 73 per cent of the vote.[1] Zelenskyy's mandate was to reboot peace talks, end the war with Russia-backed separatists in eastern Ukraine, and dismantle and detach the cronyism and the corrupt oligarchic system from Ukrainian governance.[2] By early 2021, Zelenskyy had made some progress in cracking down on pro-Russian/Ukrainian oligarchs, including Viktor Medvedchuk, a close friend of Putin. But Zelenskyy's headway, and the continued interactions with the West, only provoked Putin, who ramped up the deployment of troops on the Ukrainian borders. Putin claimed that Russians and Ukrainians were 'one people'[3] and blamed the West for initiating a 'forced change of identity' in Ukraine.[4] By December 2021, Putin had amassed tens of thousands of Russian troops to the borders in a warning to the West, demanding that Ukraine never be admitted to NATO – a request rejected by the US administration.[5]

As tension increased, and just five days before Russia's invasion, on 19 February 2022, Olaf Scholz, the German chancellor, was quoted to have told Zelenskyy to renounce his 'NATO aspirations and declare neutrality as part of a wider security deal between the West and Russia'.[6] Though Zelenskyy's electoral remit had been to eradicate corruption and enable peace across the country, particularly in the Donbas, in additional literature, Putin claimed the West had instigated an 'anti-Russia project', claiming that only 'true sovereignty of Ukraine was possible only in partnership with Russia'.[7] Following this further breakdown of relations with NATO and the West in late February, Putin instead instated the territories Donetsk and Luhansk as independent states and sent troops in to 'keep the peace'. Days before the invasion, in a speech on 21 February, Putin called Ukraine a 'Soviet creation' and questioned the legitimacy of Ukrainian statehood.[8]

Days after recognising the breakaway territories, Russia launched a full-scale invasion of Ukraine on 24 February 2022, initially at first through the eastern Ukrainian territory of Donbas. Zelenskyy declared martial law in Ukraine and officially broke diplomatic ties with Russia. Putin expected to take Ukraine quickly, as it was thought that the Russians would be 'welcomed',[9] but a hostile defence of Ukrainian territory ensued which has since been politically and economically supported by the United States and the United Kingdom, as well as the EU.[10] This kickstarted the military-industrial complex (see Chapter 1) because the invasion did immediate wonders for stocks and shares among the big American arms producers, such as Lockheed Martin, Raytheon, General Dynamics and Northrup Grumman – many of which received contracts to produce the arms which were then subsequently supplied to Ukraine. In the weeks after Russia's invasion, for example, the market capitalisation of Raytheon Technologies increased from US$128 billion to US$155 billion, while Lockheed Martin, which started 2022 worth US$98 billion, was worth US$127 billion by the end of 2022 – its highest since records began.[11]

Exodus

Thereafter began Europe's largest forced migration since the Second World War,[12] and millions of Ukrainians quickly moved from regions directly affected by the conflict to safer areas within the country while millions more left completely.[13] According to the United Nations High Commissioner for Refugees, in the first months of the war, 8.2 million people left Ukraine and around eight million were internally displaced.[14] Western politicians and media lauded the inexperienced and improvised yet brave Ukrainian soldiers while there was next to no word of NATO's build-up in the area and the US-funded specialised training of around 10,000 Ukrainian troops a year.[15] Perhaps as part of the political efforts to attach Ukraine to the EU, the Ukrainians were also depicted by the same factions as 'high-quality immigrants' because they were 'intelligent and educated' and, in the words of one French politician, 'not [part of] the refugee wave we have been used to, people with unclear pasts who could have been terrorists'. Such depictions and descriptions were widespread in the West. In another example, the British conservative columnist, Daniel Hannan, said how he was 'shocked because these are people who watch Netflix and have Instagram accounts'.[16]

Additional tension was stoked as Western media framed Russia as the 'enemy', while Russian media singled out the West as 'oppressors'. Indeed, such coverage, particularly across the West, continued 'to implement a regime of propaganda that misinformed the public and could only be perceived by Russia as an affront to the national character of its people'.[17] Within a matter of days, Valentin's Russian family stopped talking to him and ceased their communications. He tells me:

> [T]his has happened to us, from their point of view, we are part of the enemy as the West started the war. Yesterday I wrote to my niece with whom I have a basic contact but we used to be closer. She is the only one in my whole family who will respond to me. Everyone else? They think we are traitors. (Valentin)

Natasha adds that '[t]he propaganda is very strong in Russia, it's no wonder. They learn lies in school, it changes history. All this stuff like "You have to defend your country with your life"'.

Ukrainian peacekeeping personnel were required to return home, and families were separated as men of fighting age were required to remain if required for the war cause.[18] The profile of the new refugees that flooded into Europe therefore tended to be generally well-educated young women, and women with children/families.[19] They left, however, having experienced high levels of psychological distress, depressive symptoms, anxiety[20] and post-traumatic stress disorder.[21] And the arrival of millions of new refugees to European countries not only raised issues relating to their housing, economic and social integration but also whether respective nation states' infrastructures and health systems – already crippled by years of austerity and the mismanagement of the COVID-19 pandemic[22] – could support an influx of people with such difficulties.[23]

While some took advantage of protection programmes offered by the United States and Canada, most predominantly left Ukraine with Europe in mind even if some EU countries, like Spain, had no immediate plan or support infrastructure. For some years now as well, labour and skills shortages have been on the rise in all EU member states, meaning that there would almost certainly be work opportunities.[24] Europe was also preferred because of its physical proximity to Ukraine but also because the EU's Temporary Protection Directive was activated for the first time since its approval in 2001, which permitted Ukrainians immediate protection and granted them temporary work and residence permits. Ukrainians were already exempt from visa applications to the Schengen area, and it was this which facilitated the formation of Ukrainian communities in the member states prior to the conflict.[25] Eurostat data indicates that in March 2023, just over a year after the conflict, four million Ukrainians gained temporary protection and became residents in the EU, including 1.03 million in Germany, 994,000 in Poland and 448,000 in the Czech Republic.[26] Large-scale surveys show that such countries were preferred by Ukrainians because they had family members there[27] and/or wanted to be able to return regularly to their country, which importantly affected 'their willingness to apply for temporary protection schemes that oblige them to remain in destination countries'.[28]

The arrival of millions of Ukrainians in Poland resulted in emergency legislative changes to enable integration, crisis management and the general coordination of the whole country.[29] Poland was the country where most Ukrainians went because of already established migrant pathways, easier childcare arrangements and language transferability.[30] This, as well as the proximity of the country to Ukraine, was an additional feature for their migration there. This didn't necessarily dissolve immediate issues relating to skill mismatches in the economy, for most Ukrainian refugees were highly educated yet most found initial work in basic manual labour jobs.[31]

In Germany, a country which had previously welcomed hundreds of thousands of refugees when countries like Syria and Afghanistan imploded,[32] the doors were flung open once more. With an abundance of employment centres, accreditation agencies at which professional qualifications could be recognised and German language courses,[33] even though Ukrainians had in pre-war conditions taken longer to settle, they gained better paid work in comparison to other migrant groups.[34] Like Poland, those willing to stay were more likely to look for work even if many more were expecting, and hoping, to return to Ukraine.[35] Research shows, however, that this didn't seem to be the case as much for those over the age of 30 who hadn't been born in an independent Ukraine.[36] By the same measure, in the Czech Republic, Ukrainians exploited previous immigration links such as family members who moved there and areas where there were work opportunities.[37] Jobs seemed to be in abundance and 70,000 Ukrainians quickly found work by exploiting significant gaps in the labour market, and even though some young children struggled with integration in schools, surveys indicated that they tended to settle and feel welcome in the country.[38]

Spain was recently estimated to have offered temporary citizenship to around 170,000 Ukrainians since the start of the conflict and was the EU country with the fifth highest number of temporary protection permits granted. A total of 63 per cent of the people who obtained this temporary protection were women (105,998) and 37 per cent were (mostly young) men (62,133). By age group, 33 per cent were under 18; 26 per cent were between 19 and 35; 34 per cent were between 36 and 64; and 7 per cent were over 65.[39] Within the first month of the conflict, it was estimated that only 25,000 arrived, 9,000 of which registered with the authorities for 'official' help such as housing.[40] Their decision to come to Spain looked likely to have been related to the perceived generosity of its citizens[41] coupled with already established family or friend links.[42] People in this book understandably, however, seemed oblivious to the numerous infrastructural barriers awaiting them. First, Spanish housing stock is in drastically short supply, which makes rental prices high, and, second, there are limited opportunities in the formal labour market.[43] Initially, some Ukrainians were sheltered in empty hotels, some of which were left dormant in the aftermath of the COVID-19 pandemic, only to be asked to leave when paying tourists started to arrive in the summer of 2022.[44] A sizeable number, unknown because of the few who registered with the official support programme, found shelter with thousands of Spanish families who offered to host them.

Why hosting?

Because Europeans were exposed to Western media's 24-hour live coverage of the Russian invasion, it was perhaps unsurprising that many sympathised and identified with the Ukrainians' plight in their struggle against the Russians,[45] and perhaps even less unsurprising that spontaneous, grassroots effort to help Ukrainians in distress mobilised themselves across the continent.[46] This 'solidarity mobilisation',[47] unlike the period some years earlier which had seen a large-scale influx of Syrians into Europe,[48] attracted support from citizens from all over the political spectrum and among social media online forums.[49] EU states may have initially pledged to support Ukraine and its fleeing citizens, but the reality was that numerous countries were inadequately prepared to house and protect the volume of people flooding into Europe, which is why 'spontaneous initiatives of members of the public, acting as individuals or as organised platforms assembled ad hoc'.[50] In this respect, once again, the media were pivotal in driving the international outpouring of support:

> The way reporters humanised the plight of Ukrainian refugees evoked a truly extraordinary international response. Humanitarian aid for refugees poured in by the billions from governments, aid agencies and individual donors. Thousands of good-hearted people made their way to the border towns with hot meals ... to the amazement of the global community that works to help refugees, millions of refugees were relocated without the need for refugee camps because tens of thousands of local families were willing to take the displaced people into their homes.[51]

Thousands of people across Europe opened up their homes to the Ukrainians, offering temporary shelter which from lasted a few days to more long-term housing.[52] Schrooten et al's survey of 653 host family respondents in Belgium found that hosts made such gestures because they felt a 'moral duty' to do so and/or 'because society was doing too little'. They also found that Ukrainians mostly required administrative help (86.6 per cent), followed by assistance to access medical care (69.4 per cent), education (68.6 per cent), finding a more sustainable housing solution (66.7 per cent), and finding work (63.2 per cent).[53] To date, however, no study has sought to examine the length of time spent in hosts' accommodation and the impact on host and guests' mental health and wellbeing.[54] 'Positive' hosting experiences are said to relate to 'keeping to agreements' made between hosts and guests and the 'hospitableness' of a host.[55] There are, however, numerous other issues pertaining to hosting which don't feature much in the literature. One exception is a French psychotherapist, who wrote how:

The host will be confronted with various factors that they have not taken into account: although they are aware of what is happening in Ukraine, they are not really aware of the reality on the ground and the difficult journey their hosts have to make to arrive in the host country. Many Ukrainian refugees have adjustment and mental health problems such as alcoholism or personality disorders or post-traumatic stress disorder, they have a different history and culture, the notion of freedom differs between Eastern and Western Europe, gender roles are not the same everywhere. They arrive and have expectations imposed on them that are specific to Western European countries and must immediately adapt to them (forced adaptation, finding a job, enrolling their children in school, registering with a health insurance company …). The policy of the receiving countries requires them to integrate into other codes and laws as soon as they arrive, without allowing them to really breathe and digest what has just happened to them. From one trauma (fleeing war), they move on to a second trauma (adapting).[56]

Far from familiar support networks, this doesn't discount the wide margin there is for the potential exploitation of a new displaced group either into organised crime groups and/or in informal exploitative labour markets.[57] Furthermore, staying or living with unknown hosts can give rise to possible sexual abuse/violence, much of which goes underreported because of the potential for victim-blaming and stigmatisation.[58] Two Spanish women aware of these issues, who were pivotal to the Ukrainian hosting experience in Brunete and hereafter appear more frequently in the book, were Bea and Alicia:

Bea: This was why we fell short of support [as a nation and from the government]. What the government did was, because they obviously don't want to spend too much money on this, was open a call for families to help before making available their official channels of support. What it meant was, after having taken in the families, we approach the system, it says that it can't take everyone and there is a limit. This way they are not 'refugees' for them.

Dan: Ahhhh right.

Alicia: It's a way of washing their hands of the problem [the government] after promising they were going to dedicate support!

Bea: So, what happens? We assume all the responsibility. But of course, there are no checks. No one knows if someone is an abuser, a violator, whatever issues they have.

Alicia: They closed the programme quickly in any case.

Bea: It's a question of numbers. There is not enough space to be accommodated through government channels so if we, as families, assume the refugees as part of a 'humanitarian response' they wash their hands of all responsibility. So, what happened is we then assumed the responsibility for everything.

The hosts I came to know, like Bea and Alicia, may have had a clue about the possible problems arising from hosting but didn't really consider all the potential issues when they opened their doors to house Ukrainian families. Nor did I. Instead, such risks and challenges seemed to slowly dawn on us as the 'hosting experience' progressed (Chapter 3, 4 and 5). In Brunete, throughout the time we hosted, we were never told how to go about 'hosting' or heard about national strategies to integrate Ukrainians, how to help them or what to do. Big promises were made by the Spanish government, eager to show its compassion and solidarity for the new cause. Pedro Sánchez, Spain's president, was quoted as saying early on in the conflict that 'we are going to give them all the protection and opportunities possible, so that they feel at home', while the Minister for Inclusion, Social Security and Migration, José Luis Escrivá, emphasised that 'we are setting an example of collaboration, cooperation and institutional coordination, which echoes the current need for solidarity among all the citizens of Barcelona, Catalonia and Spain with the refugees from Ukraine'.[59]

Empty political promises. We searched government websites for some time about guidance and found nothing. Even as I write this book it startles me to learn that a public–private partnership existed between the Ministry of Inclusion, Social Security and Migration and La Caixa Foundation for Spanish host families. Yet none of us had heard about it or were made aware of it and, to date, there is no trace of how this venture helped the Ukrainians. When we phoned government offices, no one knew about it or about government support opportunities. It should be noted that national government websites are a maze to navigate and even phoning government helplines can be a lottery, often dependent on how helpful civil servants are feeling on that day, in that precise moment, if and when they pick up the phone. For these reasons, among others, the administrative machinery that operates housing, health, education, social security and economic affairs in Spain is immensely bureaucratic and woefully inefficient. For example, while many countries had instigated emergency laws and mobilised policy support for Ukrainian refugees, by comparison it took the Spanish government over a month just to set up the main reception, care and referral centre, to where we – as hosts – were eternally transporting the Ukrainians to and from for their respective appointments to collect temporary ID and, with a bit of luck, to be placed on a waiting list for housing. Alicia and Bea reflected on the experience:

Alicia: The arrival of the Ukrainian refugees was unreal; they shouldn't have arrived like they did. It was something between badly organised and not organised. There was no real recognised structure. The [Spanish] government gave their support to Ukraine in the political speeches but really didn't do enough for the number of people who arrived here [in Spain]. Your book should be less about our experience and more about how [it] should have been organised.

Bea: There was no one to mediate their family issues and the issues which came up with us and this was on top of problems they had from leaving their country.

Alicia: There was almost no support, no information about what to do if there were problems, no one to call. We just sort of improvised.

It is important here to note that such political cynicism is high among people in Brunete and criticisms such as these are widespread, reflecting the general disorientation and disgust the populace has with politics and the political system. Alicia and Bea aren't the only ones, for a recent national study found that 90 per cent of the public distrust political parties and 73 per cent distrust government. Perhaps making the link between these entities and new media, the same study found that 70 per cent of people in Spain also distrust the media.[60] The origins of these feelings can be linked back to Spain's introduction to Western democratic politics, globalisation and free market capitalism.[61] Since its democratic birth in 1976, Spain has embraced these ideologies and, consequently, over the decades, has come to experience increasing problems related to growing inequality, unemployment, austerity, insecure work and housing, and a crumbling healthcare system. Political party after political party, both left and right, have failed to quell the increase in these problems.[62] The townsfolk in Brunete are critical of these things and there is, if you like, a silent but resolute anti-government feeling among them. Perhaps this is because many of them see problems of unemployment, inadequate housing and insecure work opportunities around them, if not experience them directly. It could also in part stem from the days of the Spanish Civil War in the 1930s, when, in defence of the Republican cause, thousands were killed and the whole town was flattened during an ongoing conflict with government Nationalists led by General Franco in the famous Battle for Brunete in 1937. Or perhaps they express this cynicism because they feel politically disaffected after so many years of inaction over the deep-seated problems facing Spain.[63] It could, of course, be a combination.

The town we know nowadays was rebuilt during the 1940s with its centre and main square (known as 'Plaza Mayor') reconstructed and restored in tandem with the Spanish Renaissance Herreran style: a style which retained themes of austerity and minimalist decoration. Until the 1970s, many of its 1,000 or so residents mainly worked in agriculture across the surrounding land – much like its medieval founders, some nomads from Segovia known as 'Brunetas' – and hence Brunete – who were known to work the land dressed in thick, black clothes. Steady population increases were observed from the 1990s in this small, conservative working-class enclave which practically doubled in size when a bus service connected it with Madrid during a period of increased immigration to Spain at the turn of the 21st century. Together, this then attracted newly arrived immigrant groups to cheap housing for people competing for work in the domestic, construction or service sectors – similarly looking for opportunities as foreign as well as Spain's national domestic rural economies subsided.[64]

The arrival of new migrant groups reshuffled the ideological socio-economic pecking order since many local Spanish families owned local land and properties which had increased in value. Conversely, the newly arrived immigrants, like Valentin and Natasha, were working in low-wage and often exploitative conditions. And this has been the status quo ever since. Around 10,000 people live in Brunete but precarious work and unemployment is high among the immigrant population. Just over 10 per cent of the town (n=1,100) are unemployed, and the bulk of these people are from Romania, Morocco and various Latin America countries. Unless a prospective worker is prepared to travel to the wealthier nearby towns of Boadilla Del Monte, Villaviciosa de Odón or even Pozuelo De Alarcón (additionally circled in Figure 2.1), local opportunities for work are limited – particularly if you don't have your own transport or can't afford public transport. Indeed, while Brunete's neighbouring towns are blessed with direct train, metro and even tram links to the capital, such investment has not been made in Brunete, which has meant that the socio-economic profile of the residents has shifted little over the years.

Much of the town's commercial potential disappeared in the 1990s when its only shopping centre ran aground in debt and disrepair, forcing all the businesses to abandon their enterprise because consecutive political administrations were reluctant to invest in its maintenance. With its demise went more local businesses on the high street as people found fewer reasons to spend money in their local area. While there were efforts to rekindle commercial activity in 2008 with the construction of another commercial centre on the outskirts of the town, the emergence of large-scale shopping malls on the outskirts of Madrid meant that businesses soon began to pull out, including SuperCor, one of Spain's most prominent supermarket chains. The desertion was completed in 2013 when a fire in one of the remaining shops dedicated to the importation of Chinese products in the commercial centre raged across the whole complex. To this day, its ruinous and charred appearance is complemented only by daring young graffiti artists who brave

Figure 2.1: Map of Madrid in relation to Brunete, Boadilla, Villaviciosa and Pozuelo

Source: Map data © 2024 Google

the police cordons and high metal fencing to leave their colourful artworks or aimless signatures.

The failure of these ventures, coupled with the lack of investment, has forced many young people to leave. The town's ageing population thus increasingly rely on the manual and domestic workforce of revolving immigrants. Efforts to reverse this, however, were made in 2019, when the council installed a Fire Service and Civil Protection training facility to cater for up to 240 students seeking such a career.[65] It is rare to see even 10 per cent of this capacity at the centre though. Instead, the odd grouping of potential male candidates with the same haircut tend to hang around smoking cannabis before their training sessions and can be seen late at night racing each other drunkenly on their electric scooters around the backstreets. When residents complain to the authorities the most effective intervention the local police have is to drive around with blue lights flashing for 30 minutes until everyone goes home.

Other than that, life kind of carries on really. Local corruption is commonplace between politicians and police, the political mismanagement of the town's coffers continue, and Brunete's council is €16 million in debt.[66] Over the last few years, hundreds of thousands of euros were spent on a new playground (which was deemed unsafe and closed) and a new municipal swimming pool (which was built on unsafe land and closed).[67] Crime is low unless you count the last drunk man shouting obscenities out of the local bar or petty drug dealing exchanges on select street corners. The town's annual festivities attract rides and attractions for a weekend then things quieten down for 363 days. Resident families take their children to the town's park which I overlook from my flat. The town rarely hits the news unless you count a famous initiative undertaken by the local council some years back to tackle a perceived increase in dog shit on the streets. The intervention involved identifying the offending dogs and posting their shit through the owners' letterboxes. Local reports indicated that dog shit on the streets was reduced by 70 per cent[68] – some success in what is otherwise a town suffering from the consequences of free market capitalism. From shit politicians to the shit the dogs leave on the street, the hallmarks of neoliberalism are present in Brunete and the local residents complain but feel impotent to change things, instead opting for an existence which disavows the neglect and their own powerlessness (Chapter 1). A diminishing electorate continue to vote conservative but, even then, little changes and the complaints go no further than bar and café murmur.

Becoming hosts

Both Bea and Alicia had been volunteering for the local Red Cross service in Brunete prior to the Russian invasion of Ukraine. Bea, a former local schoolteacher, is now a local housing entrepreneur, having benefited from a small, post-pandemic housing construction project on the town's outskirts. Alicia is a retired social worker, totally disillusioned with the government largely because of the failures and cuts to key services she witnessed in her sector over the course of her career. Together they found great meaning and moral duty in delivering voluntary support sessions to vulnerable people and victims of domestic abuse. Prior to any Ukrainian arrivals, therefore, they already had a *propensity to help*. Their avenues into hosting, however, were slightly different. Alicia's experience relates directly to Valentin and began when he decided to drive to Poland to collect his family and personally escort them to Spain (see Figure 2.2):

> I borrowed a people carrier and drove to Poland. They were all at the border, 11 people from our family. I drove to meet them and collect them all, and for the first week or two of the conflict, we had 16 people in our three-bedroom flat. It was like sardines [laughs]. (Valentin)

When the families moved in with Valentin and Natasha in late February/early March 2022, they then contacted the local mayor. Predicting there would be further arrivals, they explained that the town council would have to do something:

> In the living room, there were five, another bedroom four, another bedroom five, like that and you had to queue for the bathroom. I was calling the mayor saying about it and how there would be more. We left message after message asking if there were Spanish families who

could take some people. But it was all last minute, no one knew what to do, on top of it in this small town which no one has heard of outside Madrid. The mayor told us to take them to the national police offices and get their papers, then contacted people she knew, of course we know now, the two who were trying to set up the association, Alicia and Bea. So, two of our families moved out. The next day, the mayor said another local Spanish woman had received a Ukrainian family, it was Bea in the end. (Natasha)

In a fluster, and concerned about potentially using up precious local funds, the mayor then contacted a trusted and active ally in the political sphere, Alicia, whom, without much thought, quickly agreed to reduce Valentin and Natasha's overpopulated flat by taking Olena, her mum and her three children, Katya, Artem and Andrei. After Alicia had managed to persuade her reluctant husband, Alberto, they all moved in, and makeshift mattresses were laid out and a sofa installed in their attic.

Bea, conversely, had a separate experience. Moved by the circumstances of the Ukrainians and the news reports of millions of people leaving the country as it went to war (Chapter 1), she contacted a friend of hers in Poland. She asked her friend if she could help and if her friend could take in a family with the intention of sending them on to where she lived in Spain. Her friend agreed and, within a few days, Tanya, Sofia aged 17 and Zlata aged 10 had temporarily moved in with her friend in Poland. 'We didn't give it a great deal of thought', said Bea, because 'we wanted to help'. 'I guess we wanted a family as we are an open family and I have three children aged nine, 11 and 14 who I thought could support whichever children we received.' After a flurry of messages, she said 'we had some conversations [with the Ukrainians] and after a few days, we paid for their tickets to come to Madrid'.

Yet there was still an awkward overcrowding in Valentin and Natasha's flat, made more difficult by the fact that both their mothers had migrated

Figure 2.2: Initial arrivals (February/early March 2022)

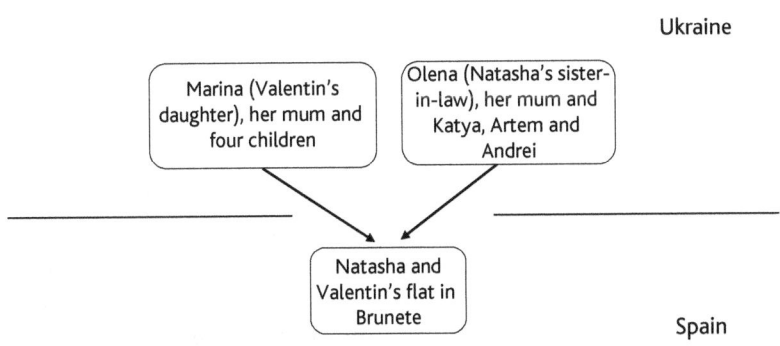

to Spain (having never left the country), didn't understand the way of life, didn't speak the language and had complex care needs relating to their elderly state. Natasha called her friend, Belén, whom she had come to know while their children were at the local school and who lived only a few streets away, asking for a favour. Before Belén even had a chance to talk to her husband, Enrique, she had already agreed to take in Marina and her four children (aged 13, nine, four and six months). Belén had already registered her interest to become a host with the regional government, the Communidad de Madrid, but had heard nothing so was very enthusiastic to help directly. Being religious, she felt it was important that, 'when it happened', 'I thought we have to help in this war and it was the best way to help to take them in'.

Website

Then where might I fit into all this? At the time, and maybe like Alicia, Bea and Belén, I didn't think too much about it either but I guess I advertised to support Ukrainian refugees because I had been in situations previously of potentially helping people 'under study' and felt I hadn't done enough. Some years ago, I undertook a three-year ethnographic project into the refugee exodus into Europe and interviewed 110 refugees from places like Iraq, Syria and Afghanistan. During the project, I came to know three young men from Syria and witnessed first-hand their social rejection and struggles to integrate in Spain. I had first interviewed them on the borders of Europe in North Africa and then followed their (mis)fortunes as they filed for asylum in Spain. They waited for months as their asylum application was decided and, in the process, experienced high levels of racism, hate and abuse from the local community in Córdoba while receiving piecemeal language courses, and substandard housing and healthcare. When they were eventually told they could only gain temporary stay for six months, they decided that Spain had no future for them and, much like their clandestine entry, returned through similar networks to Syria as if they had never existed. A month later, I was told by one of them that the other two had been killed during an ambush on their temporary residence in Aleppo, which he survived.

Since then, and in all my projects, I have made it my business to at least try to help people no matter how grave their circumstances. As I was alluding to in the first chapter, I think we have much more of a moral duty to those we study. So, when Russia's invasion took place, media news presenters with bulletproof vests from the world's most renowned television channels descended on Ukraine in an effort to boost their hopes of winning an award by delivering emotive, uncomfortable and obtuse live coverage of a country under attack. Everyday people, likely caught up in the ideologically charged maelstrom, made donations, raised Ukrainian flags in solidarity, marched in protest in public spaces and generally submitted to the latest crisis to be excessively broadcast. Within a week of the invasion, I was sent a link to a charitable website which was asking people to register as 'hosts' to receive Ukrainians in their homes. With limited space in my three-bedroom flat in Brunete, I signed up and was a little surprised that, within a few days, I had been contacted by a family of four: Oksana and her ten-year-old son, Maksym, along with her two god-daughters, Anastasia ('Nastia' hereafter) and Masha. They wanted safe haven quickly and asked if I could provide it. After a flurry of messages, we quickly arranged a videocall:

> The line finally connects after the fifth attempt and the screen comes up. I can see from left to right, Oksana, Nastia, Masha, Maksym, Dima and Oksana's mother. The light is dim, and it feels like I am about to give them a job interview for a post which we already know they have got: in less than a week, most of the family I now see online will be moving in with me. They crowd around the laptop webcam, and in the background, a few packed bags line the doorway. After a short pause, Dima speaks. 'Daniel, can you hear us? The connection is bad, but I hope we can at least have this videocall' he says in a low tone before getting up, clad in makeshift khaki clothes, to adjust the camera to get all six of the cramped figures into better view. He makes a wry smile as he sits down again, moving aside the large dagger-type knife he has attached to the belt. Soon he will have to say a painful goodbye to his family without knowing if and when he will ever see them again. We have spent the last week or so communicating through Facebook messenger as a consequence of an advert I put on a website offering shelter for Ukrainian families. The feeling is sombre as we sort of go over the details of when and how they will arrive before Dima says for the 20th time 'Daniel, thank you very, very much for doing this for my family'. The drawn-out goodbye is quickly shortened as the air raids start up. A few seconds later, and with a fist in the air, he adds '*Slava Ukraïni*' [meaning Glory to Ukraine] and hangs up the call. (Field notes, '*Slava Ukraïni*')

Notes

[1] Gomza (2022).
[2] Benjamin and Davies (2022).
[3] Varshalomidze (2019).
[4] Putin (2021).
[5] Eichensehr (2022).
[6] Abelow (2022: 58).
[7] Putin (2022).
[8] Gomza (2022).
[9] Johnson (2022).

10. Trebesch et al (2023).
11. Rashid (2023).
12. Gromadzki and Lewandowski (2022).
13. Panchenko (2022).
14. UNHCR (2022).
15. Benjamin and Davies (2022).
16. Benjamin and Davies (2022).
17. Abelow (2022: 50).
18. Johnson (2022).
19. Panchenko (2022); Brücker et al (2023).
20. Buchcik et al (2023).
21. Rizzi et al (2022); Catani et al (2023).
22. Briggs et al (2021; 2023).
23. Jankowski and Gujski (2022); Murphy et al (2022); Spiegel (2022).
24. European Commission (2024).
25. Enríquez (2022).
26. Eurostat (2023).
27. Panchenko (2022).
28. Andrews et al (2023: 1).
29. Lee et al (2023).
30. Babakova et al (2022).
31. Gromadzki and Lewandowski (2022).
32. Briggs (2020).
33. Panchenko and Poutvaara (2022).
34. Brücker et al (2023).
35. Panchenko and Poutvaara (2022); Molikevych (2023).
36. Panchenko (2022).
37. Adunts et al (2022).
38. Lintner et al (2023); Molikevych (2023).
39. *La Moncloa* (2023).
40. Escrivá (2022).
41. Spanish citizens rank first in the world in their individual contributions to the UNHCR (Global Attitudes Survey, 2018).
42. UNHCR (2022).
43. Enríquez (2022); Koroutchev (2023).
44. Terol (2022).
45. Enríquez (2022); Politi et al (2023).
46. Babakova et al (2023).
47. Carlsen et al (2023).
48. Briggs (2020).
49. Carlsen and Toubøl (2023); Carlsen et al (2023).
50. Enríquez (2022: 5).
51. Benjamin and Davies (2022: 120–1).
52. Dunn and Kaliszewska (2023).
53. Schrooten et al (2023).
54. Duray-Parmentier (2023).
55. Altinay et al (2023); Schrooten et al (2023).
56. Duray-Parmentier (2023: 273).
57. Pertek et al (2022).
58. Rodriguez (2022).

59 *La Moncloa* (2022).
60 De la Fuente and Pinilla (2023).
61 Winlow et al (2015).
62 Winlow et al (2015).
63 Winlow et al (2015).
64 Briggs and Monge Gamero (2017).
65 TeleMadrid (2019).
66 See, for example, TeleMadrid (2017; 2020).
67 TeleMadrid (2023).
68 TeleMadrid (2013).

3

'We are not refugees! We are occupiers!'

In the messages that follow, and perhaps eager to ensure Maksym has something in place for during-the-day activities, Oksana discreetly tells me how she has been able to get him a basketball scholarship in a small academy in the south of Madrid. Likely persuaded by his height but more so by the financial contributions to the academy, the coach permits Maksym to join on his arrival in Spain. In this chapter, Oksana's family's journey is charted and their early introduction to Spain and Spanish cultural life is documented. On their arrival, my small hometown was simultaneously swelling with other Ukrainian guests so segments of their life in Ukraine and their journey are also described here, giving particular attention to the Russian invasion and their immediate departure from their country.

Welcome to Spain!

The continued threat to Kyiv was enough for Oksana to decide to leave the country with Maksym and her two god-daughters, Nastia and Masha. After a long trek out of Poland, during which the family got stuck in hundred-kilometre traffic jams which extended to the Polish border, they made their emotional farewells and continued onward. All the while, as Oksana recalls, they were 'stuck in their own living nightmare'. More than anything, Oksana struggled to give explanations to Maksym who was constantly asking questions about why he had to leave his father and the rest of his family, his home, his school and his whole life; the only reason to which she kept referring was to better his potential for a career as a basketball player. The family made slow progress to Warsaw where they rested for a few days with another host family found on the same website before taking a flight to Madrid. In the absence of school, and to ease the sudden change, Oksana was eager to get something in place for Maksym. Before arrival, they had made contact with a basketball academy in the south Madrid area and had exchanged some videocalls. The manager had almost no hesitation in inviting the tall Maksym to a few trial sessions on arrival in Spain; it's certainly difficult to ignore the fact that Maksym is my height (1.75 metres) and he is only ten. The manager agreed to take Maksym into the youth team, thus aiding Oksana's wishes to soften the sudden departure because of war and instead present the move to Spain as an opportunity, as something for his sporting benefit and future. It was here that the family stopped again with another host family found on the same website for a few nights.

All this took place over the course of a week, and my address was their final destination. Meanwhile, I was frantically tidying and reorganising my flat. I first moved my daughter's (Nadia's) clothes and belongings out of her wardrobe and into my room, took out the spare single bed underneath and bought new sheets. This room was to be where Oksana and Maksym would sleep. The next cleaning project was the spare double bedroom where Nastia and Masha would sleep. Once again, I bought more new sheets and new towels and toothbrushes but didn't want to turn it too much into a charity affair or a hotel experience so went no further. Anticipating that they would want space in the cramped kitchen, I cleaned out two shelves in the fridge and a whole cupboard before giving the whole flat a deep clean. *I was as ready as I could have been* I thought.

Only then did it quickly dawn on me that I would not only need to be managing my own adaptation to a situation of hosting four unknown people but that of Nadia's as well. Yet the imminence of their arrival didn't seem to faze her. I remember how I briefed her one day after school by telling her that 'next Monday, we will probably be collecting some people to stay with us, they had to leave their country because of war'. The concept of war for an eight-year-old is not easy to understand but I explained that they had left where they live because it was dangerous and there was a risk to their lives. Nadia seemed open and enthusiastic to the prospect, maybe because she exhibited the same level of excitement and curiosity when she was three and accompanied me in refugee camps and social housing projects in the suburbs of Paris during an earlier project.[1] She was soon to be sharing a small space with another young boy who didn't speak her language. 'We will be able to play together', she said to me confidently, as I collected her from school in the week preceding their arrival. Believe me, there is nothing more heartwarming than how innocently a child can smooth over a potentially complicated situation.

And the closer the collection date came, the more I realised just how complicated it could be. By now Oksana and her family had arrived in Madrid and, having secured Maksym's academy place and met the manager, were lodging for another few nights with another Spanish host in Boadilla Del Monte, the neighbouring town. This was to be their last stop until I could collect them since I had been at a conference prior to their arrival. In the car, on the day I went to meet them, I remember I just kept telling myself to *take it day by day*. During the journey to collect them, Nadia looked out of the window and asked me questions about our new guests that I didn't know how to answer. When we pulled up outside the Spanish host family's house, out came Oksana, Maksym, Nastia and Masha, and Nadia and I greeted and embraced them all. Masha was to stay for a night or two more with the temporary hosts to see if there was a potential work opportunity in a nearby restaurant and I was to collect her a few days later. My small car struggled to pull away under the added weight as they talked among themselves in Ukrainian. 'We are safe', said Oksana as we turned out of the neighbouring town of Boadilla Del Monte. I kept looking discreetly in the mirror at Oksana, studying her mannerisms as she spoke. It was 5.12pm on Monday 28 March 2022 and for all of us life was changing once again.

Oksana, Maksym, Nastia and Masha

We parked outside the flat and I helped them up the stairs with their luggage and gave them a quick guided tour of my compact but humble flat. Things seemed more spacious in the pictures I had sent them as my place quickly filled with these new people and their belongings. The view from my living room overlooks the town's main park where sit various climbing frames, a basketball court and small football pitch. *It would be ideal for Maksym and Nadia*, I thought, *at least to get to know each other*. The flat sits above an educational school and close to a Moroccan supermarket but is within easy walking distance of all the amenities. *This would be convenient for Oksana, Nastia and Masha should they need anything if I was away*, I thought. They started to unpack, and I started to make dinner, giving them privacy to make calls to Ukraine. Nadia showed Maksym her room and tried to find things for him to play with; the best they seemed to do was with a 'guess who' game, which, with the aid of Google Translate, became pretty amusing for both of them.

None of my new guests had tried English food but they all politely finished it. When I made Spanish dishes, it similarly didn't feel right either. After a few days, they offered to cook for me. It didn't take long for them to share their stories of the invasion. Though cold at night in the transit countries through which they travelled, they explained how they slept with the shutters open, still in fear that planes loaded with bombs were circling overhead. Only one month previously, Russian forces had invaded their country and targeted the capital, Kyiv, as one of the early sites for victory. Initially, the Russians seized key areas to the north and west of Kyiv, which led many commentators to predict that the city would fall imminently. Robust Ukrainian resistance, however, exhausted the Russian momentum and this, coupled with poor Russian strategy and weak tactical decisions, denied the 'occupiers' a potential encirclement.

Citizens were also told to avoid windows and balconies for fear of sniper shots as the potential onslaught started to become more visible. Satellite images, for example, revealed how Putin's tanks could be seen tailing back over 50 kilometres from a motorway stretch north of the city. Infrastructural targets such as industrial silos and media institutions were targeted and, in early March, the Kyiv Tower, which emitted TV and radio throughout the region, was obliterated by missiles. The Ukrainian resistance was strong, nevertheless, and by mid-March 2022, had started to push back Russian forces from segments of the city's neighbourhoods.

After a month of intense fighting, the Ukrainian forces began counterattacking and pushed back the Russians. In fact, the day after their arrival in my flat, 29 March 2022, signalled the full retreat of Russian forces from Kyiv. Only four days later, the whole area and its surrounding domain fell back under the control of the Ukrainians. Oksana saw first-hand the remnants of the battle for Kyiv. 'I don't think we could believe it either', said Oksana. 'I mean we heard gunfire and explosions in our district and one day, when I managed to get the bravery together, I went on to the street to get provisions from a shop, and saw an abandoned Russian tank.' Attempts were made by the Russians to sever electricity to the city and a curfew was introduced. Violators were considered to be 'traitors' said Nastia, 'but there was conflicting information about who was firing against who and who was bombing who and the propaganda made people wary of each other', she added. The in-reserve Ukrainian Territorial Defence Forces were called to duty and everyday citizens were also 'asked to fight' said Oksana. 'The people of the city were asked to defend it, people had to make homemade missiles [Molotov cocktails] and guns were passed around.'

When Russia did finally withdraw from the area, hundreds of people were estimated to have died on both sides. The discovery of war crimes in Bucha – a small suburban town outside Kyiv – was to further intensify the geopolitical scenario. In the aftermath of Bucha, Human Rights Watch found evidence of executions, unlawful killings, enforced disappearances and torture, and by 15 April 2022, 278 bodies had been found, most of whom were civilians.[2] Further investigations indicated the death toll to be 461.[3] The experience of Bucha, however, enraged Ukrainians even further and became one of the main symbolic catalysts for requesting further Western support and finance for the Ukrainian war efforts, thus propagating the military-industrial complex (Chapters 1 and 2). The event was to also contribute to further international media attention, which resulted in increased momentum for Western support for the Ukrainian cause (Chapter 1). Indeed, in the aftermath of the war crimes, Joe Biden was quoted as saying that 'Putin cannot stay in power' in a famous speech[4] which seemed to symbolise the US-led desire to dismantle Russia.[5]

Learning from the new live-in neighbours

Our discussions went well into the early hours of the morning over the first few nights. And in the days that followed, we communicated in broken English, and I got to know my new friends. After dropping Nadia at school, I often returned to find that Nastia and Masha had been exploring the town and Oksana had bought the day's food from the local Moroccan supermarket. One day, she declared how she wanted to make me a special Ukrainian dish. Her bag was full of vegetables minus an ingredient which was essential, or 'it make bad meal' she said. Her broken English wasn't good enough to describe to me what it was and my Ukrainian didn't go beyond 'hello' or '*pryvit*' and 'thank you' or '*dyakuyu*'. We consulted pictures on Google and still couldn't work it out before Masha finally put us out of our linguistic misery and brought up her online translation tool on her phone. We found out that Oksana was looking for 'crème fraiche' and all laughed. I then offered to bring it back from the larger supermarket. 'I'm cook for you today', Oksana said proudly. 'You will love', she told me, as she started to explore my kitchen for the things she needed to prepare it all.

Borshch, pronounced 'Boorsh' – a predominantly vegetable-based Ukrainian cuisine mainly prepared with cabbage, onion and some croutons – was what Nadia and I came to try that same evening (Figure 3.1). *It's not bad*, I thought to myself, as, in the weeks that followed, Nadia and I were

Figure 3.1: Typical *Borshch* dish

to try numerous versions of *Borshch*, alternated in the main with *kotleku* (meatballs), *holubtsi* (stuffed cabbage) and the world-famous chicken Kyiv (herb-stuffed breaded chicken). What didn't seem to change was our reliance on the online translation tool. Oksana's English was good enough for me to understand what she wanted to say but her long-winded explanations slowed down the ability for us to communicate quickly and effectively. Neither of us seemed to mind and much of this was instead compensated by Nastia and Masha who had a much better command of the language. As I was to find out, this was a common feature among many of the Ukrainian families in Brunete; that the women over 40 tended to have little to no knowledge of English while the younger women had much better competency. Maksym, I figured, knew next to no English as he hadn't yet studied it at school. The best he could manage with us was 'Hello, how are you?' and high fives or fist bumps.

Conversations, both with and without the online translation tool, perhaps unsurprisingly oscillated around the evolving war, which they all seemed to follow incessantly on various media platforms. If they weren't getting updates on their mobiles, there were furiously engaged in sending messages. My TV was also hijacked by a constant stream of war updates from Ukrainian media channels; even when they weren't watching it, it was a background presence. All this directed almost all our conversations around the war:

> They [the Ukrainians] spend much time following the news and developments, which depict Russia as the enemy hence the high hate for Russia and low trust in Russians. The news stories relay reports of children being raped and women having their teeth cut out before being rolled up in carpets and burnt. During our dinners, Oksana and Nastia relay their guilt for leaving their country and being somewhere safe. Each time they hear planes overhead or loud noises, they jump and look cautious as they feel they are about to be attacked. On one such occasion when a helicopter circles the town, Nastia goes to her room, closes the door, pulls the shutters down and turns the light off and remains in the dark until the noise from the rotors desists. When she comes out an hour or so later, she explains herself and her reaction. She says it reminds her of a story in which, over a period of a week, she gradually moved down from the third floor of her parents' house to the ground floor at night because she couldn't sleep from the shelling, bombing and fighting. (Field notes, 'Depictions')

These harsh emotional and psychological scars now seemed quite normal for Nastia and the way she talked about them manifested obvious stress and suffering evidenced in various studies undertaken in Europe about Ukrainian refugee trauma.[6] But this felt very little compared to the ejected state she felt in the wake of now being 'witnesses of our own history'. At dinner, just a week into their stay, there was a heated discussion about the use of the Russian language. Ukrainians knew both languages but now reverted only to Ukrainian as there was a collective rejection of the Russian language. This led to further conversations about how Ukrainians like Nastia were living through their own history in a way which didn't directly involve them:

> Nastia says people she knows speak now more Ukrainian than Russian – 'these people did this to us so we stop speaking their language' she says as she breaks more bread. 'This wasn't the case before' she adds as people generally communicated in Russian prior to the war. As she helps herself to more Borshch, Nastia describes her life as a 'historical tutorial' in which she is 'learning about my own history as it happens, in front of the whole world'. She adds how 'we are now witnesses of our own history'. Nastia then shows me on her mobile a picture of a referee, a friend and colleague, who died fighting. She zooms in on the smiley figure who was celebrating in the wake of a sporting victory. Only a few days earlier, Oksana broke the news of how a journalist friend was killed: she says, 'it's not safe for anyone, especially those who try to report truth of what is happening to Ukrainians'. (Field notes, 'Dinner discussions')

Such an investment in following the unfolding events increased the level of 'guilt' the Ukrainians felt for leaving their country. In their work with Ukrainian refugees settling in the Czech Republic during the same period, Mazhak et al found that to counter such 'guilt', Ukrainians tried to embed themselves in other activities by means of 'taking their mind off things' which displayed a 'behavioural disengagement' after which they often returned to blaming themselves for leaving their country.[7] This significantly affected their emotional state and seemed to be increasingly aggravated during and after videocalls or phone calls with partners, family and/or friends back home. On one night within the first two weeks of their stay, I could hear Oksana crying in her room as she talked to her husband Dima in English – by means of practising – while Maksym was playing with Nadia in the living room:

> 'I miss you so much', I hear her say in a whispering tone, perhaps because she doesn't want Maksym more than anyone else to hear her in this vulnerable state. 'We have no choice at this time, we have to be apart' he says before she interrupts, 'I didn't want to leave you it was only for Maksym that I am here'. 'We must do it for him more than anyone' says Dima. Suddenly they switch to Ukrainian, and I move on through

the hallway. Then a few minutes later, Oksana comes out of the room having dried her eyes and passes me the phone. 'Dima want speak to you' she says. I take the phone into the kitchen. 'Daniel, you must know that we appreciate all your support and help, thank you for looking after my son' he says as he cries. He suddenly cuts from the call however, which we later learn was because there was an imminent air raid. (Field notes, 'Choices')

Poor refugee versus forced migrant

Ways out of feeling like this were near impossible in the early stages of Oksana and her family's stay. Similar emotional conversations were also overheard when Nastia and Masha called their parents, both of whom had declared themselves 'too old' to move country and start again. They had sold many assets to be able to fund Nastia and Masha and were resolute in their decision that it made more sense to put resources towards their children's safety than their own. By the same token, Nastia and Masha didn't want Spanish state handouts or any kind of sympathy for their situation, for as we will see, Nastia was to assume the kind of head of family role outside Ukraine as additional sacrifices fell on her shoulders for the welfare, wellbeing and future of those younger than her (see Chapter 4). They all refuted the 'refugee' label, in fact even more so when it was accompanied with any kind of reference to being 'poor' or 'needy'. On one occasion, and as a change of media scenery, I changed the TV station and put on a Spanish news channel so they could see how they were being received by the Spanish and better understand their depiction:

> I put on the automatic English subtitles, so I don't have to translate in the moment. The news reels they then watch incessantly cover the arrival of Ukrainians to Spain and there are a series of interviews with formal politicians as well as emergent helping services. Nastia starts to shake her head. 'They are talking about us as if we are poor, needy refugees' she says and fold her arms in protest. 'We don't need this treatment, for people to feel sorry for us, we are not refugees. We have jobs, education, we are independent people' she adds. Masha says, 'we are not even being invaded, it is just a temporary occupation' and laughs. 'Now we are occupying your flat' says Nastia to me and laughs louder. This, another example, of the cold yet blunt humour they apply to such situations seems to manage the trauma of their experience to date: from their immediate uprooting to the long, emotional videocalls they have into the early hours of the morning. It also seems fitting to describe the lack of agency they are assumed to have in these circumstances. 'We have to make the most of

the situation, even if we don't know what will happen' concludes Nastia. (Field notes, '*Noticias*')

As we will see, they very much do this (Chapters 4 and 5) but this determination to do something, to make the most of the situation, to refute pity or sympathy, to want to work, and so on, represented a general rejection of wanting to be treated as 'helpless victims' and to rebuff any sense of victimhood attached to their circumstances. Such resilience shown by forcibly displaced people, the literature suggests,[8] hinges on positive family and community cohesion and support, collective identity, supportive primary relationships and religion. This very much appeared to be their aim as they seemed to create their way of life as much as possible around them, so it didn't feel that they were as far away from home. They ate at the same specific times, made Ukrainian food all the time, even ironed and folded clothes as they would do at home. It felt like they were trying to ease the burden of the experience by recreating as many familiar and routine activities as possible. Having access to *Servant of the People* similarly seemed to assist in this process, as it helped them to deepen their affiliation to their comedian-turned-president, Volodymyr Zelenskyy, and almost fetishise the idea of Ukraine as a corrupt-free democratic state, liberated from the control of poisonous elite oligarchs who controlled political, cultural and social life (Chapter 1).

Servant of the People

Zelenskyy's election campaign seemed clearly linked to his popular fictional depiction of a high-school history teacher, Vasily Petrovych Goloborodko, who, in the series *Servant of the People*, is unexpectedly elected president of Ukraine after a viral video filmed by one of his students shows him ranting against government corruption in his country. The student then uploads the footage to YouTube, and Vasily, who lives with his parents, turns into an Internet sensation overnight. Vasily's students launch a crowdfunding campaign to register his candidacy in Ukraine's presidential race, unbeknownst to him, which eventually propels their flabbergasted teacher to political victory as the new president of Ukraine. While in office, Vasily becomes overwhelmed by his newfound responsibilities, but gradually eases into his presidential duties and decides to weed out oligarchic corruption in his government. For these reasons, the programme was celebrated for its critique of the pervasive corruption, inefficiency and disconnect between the government and the populace, and by addressing these issues through satire – something Slavoj Žižek would be proud of[9] – the show resonated with millions of Ukrainians, fostering a sense of collective awareness and engagement with political discourse.

Netflix made series 1 of *Servant of the People* available in March 2022 and it was what Oksana suggested we watch to help me understand Ukrainian culture and the way of life as well as get an insight into the country's president. The main elements of his political cause in the fictional depiction of Vasily Petrovych Goloborodko were to become the presidential manifesto of Zelenskyy, highlighting how the real-life crossover underscores the series' impact, demonstrating how media can shape political realities and inspire public movements. The platform of a 'series' alongside a series of selfie clips where he appears as a non-traditional and anti-establishment character had become the hallmark of Zelenskyy's political campaign and led him to a 73 per cent victory in 2019. In his victory speech, Zelenskyy said: 'I am the hope for change not just for people in Ukraine but for all people.' However, his popularity diminished in the following months before the invasion because there seemed to be no progress towards peace with Russia in the Donbas and allegations of corruption surfaced as he started to crack down on opposition parties. Consequently, citizens saw him ebbing towards the general trajectory of previous Ukrainian presidents – someone bent on sustaining their own power via corrupt means (Chapters 1 and 2). However, his appearance in the streets of central Kyiv with ministers from his government in the early part of Russia's invasion started to reverse his dipping popularity, instead converting into national unity.

Momentum in international support of Ukraine grew quickly in this early period as a feeling of unity was steadily bolstered by the negative global attention being directed at Putin and the Russian state. For the time being, the Ukrainians had seen off the Russian advances in Kyiv and Kharkiv, and there were signs for them that the Russian state may not be as intimidating as they had first thought. Even with millions of its country's citizens strewn across Europe, the nation had quickly united and repelled a world superpower, and this increased confidence levels in Zelenskyy and his government. All these signs pointed to a collective fortitude which had strengthened faith in winning the war.[10] Indeed, in this very same period in which these Ukrainians were settling in Brunete, four waves of Gradus Research self-completed surveys conducted in Ukraine from February to May 2022 showed a steady increase in national unity, trust in the president and faith in victory among the Ukrainian population.[11]

After playing with the TV settings for 20 minutes, I managed to work out how to have the audio in Ukrainian and the subtitles in English to be able to watch *Servant of the People*. We commenced the viewing one night, all packed on to the sofa. They smiled and laughed as we watched five episodes back-to-back, each time becoming more immersed in the plot as Vasily Petrovych Goloborodko clumsily ascended into government. The portrayal of an everyday person ascending to power and the influence of an 'ordinary citizen' on significant social change seemed to be the blueprint for their optimism: that disavowing the reality of war with Russia would instead keep alive the initial idealised hope that Ukraine could make peace with Russia and evict the corrupt oligarchs – just like in the series. Peace, however, seemed a long way away, affirmed by the continual arrival of more Ukrainians to my hometown.

Kharkiv, further arrivals and the expanding host network

Around the same time as Oksana's arrival to my flat more Ukrainian families descended on Brunete, in the main from Kharkiv, a Ukrainian city just 30 kilometres from the Russian border. Kharkiv had faced the immediate brunt of the Russian invasion, with troops and tanks descending on the city just two days into the conflict on 24 February 2022. Reports suggested that Kharkiv was the centre of the heaviest fighting as Ukrainian soldiers and civilians fought alongside each other to resist the Russian invasion. With relative success, the Russians were pushed back to the outskirts of the city before more intensified strikes took place from the end of February to early April 2022. Cluster bombs, missiles and rockets became the attack mode of choice as more strategic attempts were made to damage vital infrastructure as areas of the city were deprived of electricity, water and power. Hundreds of civilians and an unknown number of soldiers were killed as the airstrikes continued. Among those hiding in the basement of their block of flats were Valentyna and her family:

> Valentyna brushes aside her long blonde hair and continues to flick through the pictures on her phone. A former Miss Kharkiv winner, now a fashion designer, she had to abandon her business and shop when the Russians invaded as the surrounding neighbourhood was heavily damaged by the airstrikes. When she finally finds the image to show me, her eyes well. The photo is one her husband has taken of them crouching for safety in the basement of their block of flats; Valentyna has her arms wrapped around her daughter, Yesenia. 'This is what we had to endure night after night until one day my husband say I have to go, he gave me money and I took what I money had and I got my car and drove and drove' she recalled. 'Going out on the street, there was fighting and firing' she says, adding how 'there were tanks in the streets'. (Field notes, 'War photos')

Valentyna – who had driven to Spain with her three-year-old daughter, Yesenia, and elderly mother – had ended up in a neighbouring town, no fewer than five kilometres from Brunete. I had met her, however, through her best friend Anya and the expanding Ukrainian networks. Anya used

Figure 3.2: Further arrivals (mid-to-late March 2022)

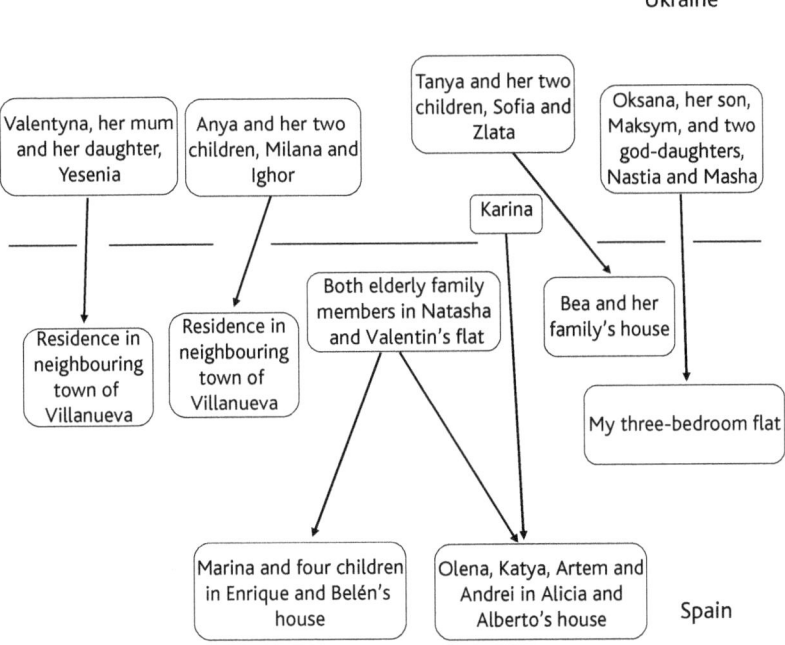

to be employed as a shop manager under Valentyna in Kharkiv. They had known each other their whole lives and went to school together. Anya, like Valentyna, found herself in the same neighbouring town in Spain with her two children, Ighor aged eight and Milana aged six.

As Figure 3.2 shows, the dynamics therefore changed early on in Valentin and Natasha's flat, with Marina moving in with Enrique and Belén and their two children, Adrian aged 15 and Cristina aged 17. Olena, a hairdresser, and her four children moved in with Alicia who we met in Chapter 2. Karina, Katya's partner, arrived shortly after and shared the same attic space in Alicia's house. Bea, who was similarly introduced in the previous chapter, assumed a family of three: Tanya, Sofia and Zlata. While I didn't meet all the Ukrainian families in Brunete, these were among the emerging group whom Oksana and I started to come to know. Like Oksana, they all felt the same about their situation: that this was something temporary and that, above everything else, they wanted and desired to go home as soon as possible. Given that it is estimated that one in three refugees suffer from high rates of depression, anxiety, and post-traumatic stress disorders,[12] it was important that the Ukrainians got access to resources and support quickly: if not, such feelings could easily be exacerbated.[13]

Notes

1. Briggs (2020).
2. Human Rights Watch (2023).
3. Harmash (2023).
4. Benjamin and Davies (2022).
5. Mearsheimer (2014; 2022).
6. Fegert et al (2018); Rizzi et al (2022).
7. Mazhak et al (2023).
8. Siriwardhana et al (2014).
9. Žižek (2009).
10. Albrecht and Panchenko (2022).
11. Gradus (2022).
12. See Turrini et al (2017).
13. Oppedal and Idsoe (2015).

4

Work, study and cultural integration

> Many Ukrainian refugees have adjustment and mental health problems such as alcoholism or personality disorders or post-traumatic stress disorder, they have a different history and culture, the notion of freedom differs between Eastern and Western Europe, gender roles are not the same everywhere. They arrive and have expectations imposed on them that are specific to Western European countries and must immediately adapt to them (forced adaptation, finding a job, enrolling their children in school, registering with a health insurance company).[1]

As this quote highlights, the reality was that many of the Ukrainian families arriving in Brunete had varying levels of mental health stresses – perhaps evidenced in Nastia's reaction to the helicopter (Chapter 3) – and were now exposed to a range of pressures from the host culture. As the dystopian honeymoon period started to diminish, Oksana and her family as well as the growing number of Ukrainians in Brunete assumed the mountainous administrative tasks that now loomed on the horizon. Relief that safety had been achieved was replaced by a panging guilt and a reluctant necessity to obtain things which symbolically confirmed they now resided in another country. It was at this point that the cultural integration began but also simultaneously started to end at the same time. In this chapter, I consider how early steps were taken towards learning the language, finding work and adapting to cultural life in Spain. Here we also therefore account for some of the other Ukrainians and their experiences in this true-to-life storybook.

Making existence formal

Oksana and her family quickly became frustrated at the bureaucratic machinery that stood between them and getting access to basic things like language classes, educational and work opportunities. The state, likely saving money because people like myself were doing goodwill deeds, provided no subsistence costs for hosting refugees, provided no clear pathway for children to access schools, and the only jobs available in many unemployment offices were poorly paid manual labour jobs on which a general pool of similar other in-limbo migrant workers were surviving. Having moved to Spain ten years ago, I had been through some of the administrative processes myself and thought this would be advantageous because I could potentially fast-track everything. I began by personally escorting them to various offices and translating for them:

> It's not long before Oksana is asking me with help to get their ID documents. On only the third day, I walk down with them to Brunete town hall and with their passports register them on the 'padron' or the local census. This is one of the easiest processes because the local town hall is never busy and census enquiries or adjustments rarely happen as the town's population is generally static. After a short wait in the census office, I am issued a document to say they are officially living with me. With that, we then go the next day to Pozuelo National Police office on the outskirts of Madrid to start to find out how to get the temporary Spanish documentation. I am familiar with the office having had to get my own identification there ten years ago. It reminded me of how, when I went there when I first moved to Spain, I was told that to get Spanish registered ID, I needed a work contract. When I went to the university to get the work contract, they told me I needed a bank account first. When I went to the bank, they told me I needed Spanish registered ID to open an account and a work contract. Such is the nature of how things are in Spain.
>
> Nastia had tried the registry hotline every day since arrival, calling at least every half an hour but the line was constantly engaged. I offer to drive them down there so we could instead present ourselves. We bundle into my small car and drive the 20km to the fringes of Madrid. Outside the office, there is a large Ukrainian flag flying high as other displaced Ukrainians arrive in waves: some in cars, some in vans, and others by the busload. But you can't just walk in and get the ID and there is a lot of confusion as, like most things related to administration in Spain, you need a 'cita previa' which means 'prior appointment'. Before the convenience of the internet, this meant physically presenting yourself to queue get an appointment to get a prior appointment. Now everything is online and supposedly more efficient. The prior appointment app, however, has crashed due to the number of people trying to use it and no one can get through on the hotline. And this is why people like us are just showing up at the doors of the National Police in their droves.
>
> Among this general fluster, the official National Police officers just calmly yet authoritatively look on below their sunglasses with folded arms over their guns. But without an appointment, no one enters the building. Some volunteer translators come out and give us the same phone number Nastia has already tried as I talk to a police officer about alternatives. 'No, you have to go through the phone number for the appointment, this is the process' the volunteer tells us as the collective morale drops quickly. Nastia bangs in the number into her phone with

her finger and calls again. I don't believe in God, but someone must have been looking kindly on us in that moment for within a minute she somehow gets through and manages to book them all appointments. The wait for the first appointment is six weeks. Documents are presented at that appointment before another appointment is required to collect the ID. Back we get into the car to return home feeling like the first of many phases is now complete. The only problem is that without the ID, none of them can formally work or have access to other social benefits. (Field notes, 'ID')

In Spain, these things need to be taken one step at a time and the motivation to get through it created a general feeling of positivity about getting the necessary documentation – even if it meant waiting. The temporary high was quelled in mid-April 2022 when Maksym's basketball scholarship ended abruptly and the basketball school, for some unknown reason, went into 'administration'. No deposit refund for Oksana. Suddenly, Maksym was just kicking around at home all day and was getting agitated and bored. Oksana had initially been reluctant to start any process of schooling, thinking and hoping that she and her family would soon be returning to Ukraine but also to minimise the amount of change for Maksym. Now, however, she felt she had little choice. Oksana and I looked at the local council website to find the address for the social security office, which was where we needed to go to register Maksym in a school:

> Even though the social security is on the same square to where I live, we have to look hard for the plaque advertising its offices. We arrive first thing after opening hours at 9.30am to ensure we get seen to but there is a notice on the door 'regreso en 15 minutos' which means 'I will return in 15 minutes'. Without knowing when this was put up, we simply wait. Five minutes pass as we look around at an array of parked cars and people having breakfast in the nearby café. Ten minutes pass as I start to lean against the door. After 15 minutes, I make a knock at the door. There is no answer. I knock again a bit harder which seems to arouse the attention of someone from the nearby café. A man gets up, chewing his food and asks us what we are doing. 'We need to see if we can get Maksym some funding for some local sports activities and register him for a place in school' I explain. 'Ah ok, let me finish my breakfast and I will see you' he says. Who would have thought it was possible for an employee responsible for opening the office to have breakfast during working hours by shutting the office in the process. This is how Spain works though. …
>
> After another ten minutes pass, the man returns, and we go in. I translate in Spanish as the man doesn't speak English or Ukrainian. 'The funding has been

cut this year for children's activities, so each child registered to live in Brunete can choose only one activity which lasts one hour per week' he explains. There are only two choices. Football or swimming. Since Maksym doesn't like football, Oksana chooses swimming. Oksana says he can swim 'a bit' but when I take Maksym to the local pool a few hours later so the swimming staff can assess his level, it doesn't seem to be too much. He gets changed and then gets in the pool only to sort of activate his arms and legs as much as possible without going anywhere. It doesn't really improve in the following 20 minutes since everything the swimming coach is saying, he doesn't understand. (Field notes, 'Sink or swim')

War games

Now that Maksym was at home in the flat, Oksana couldn't continue her online consultancy work and became more and more worried that surplus time would negatively impact her son and amplify the immediate change to his life:

> I don't know how much war games played a feature in Maksym's life pre-2022, but they seem to be what he is most interested in doing while he is at home [see Figure 4.1]. I ask him if the army is Ukrainian but he says it is 'English and American' before he strategically lines up the forces: curious

Figure 4.1: Maksym playing war games

that he doesn't recognise the Ukrainians as the soldiers. Up front there is a mix, the odd tank and soldier as if to give a sense of chaos and lack of strategy but behind the lines are rows upon rows of soldiers, ready for the battle, ready for the fight. The planes hide behind the sofa as if to take the enemy by surprise. Nadia tries to match up with her Princess dolls who seemed equally determined yet at the same time perhaps slightly out of place in a war. Maksym's surprise attacks, however, win the day. (Field notes, 'War games')

First day at school

As the days passed, Maksym's behaviour became challenging as he got more restless at home. Now the basketball opportunity was lost, he became more inquisitive into the reasons for leaving Ukraine. He understood there was conflict and danger but because his father, Dima, and his grandmother were still there, he wanted to return. Perhaps seeing me as some sort of replacement father figure, increasingly there were times where he suddenly embraced me for no reason. He also became more emotional during the videocalls with his father who, as Oksana said, 'by the luck of God', had not yet been called to fight for his country. Oksana did her best to keep Maksym active by taking him down to the basketball courts, but it didn't take long for him to get bored and frustrated. In desperation, Oksana asked that we tried other options because the lack of routine and general activity was affecting his behaviour. He was also developing sleeping problems and irritable bowel syndrome, 'likely related to the stress' the doctor said when we took him for a check-up. After making numerous unsuccessful phone calls, we went down to the local mayor's office to see if we could get him into a local school. Oksana had been reluctant because, once again, schooling may signify a more permanent stay:

> Miracles happen. But it takes the right person with the right connections to prize open the closed doors. Until yesterday, Maksym had no kind of support for anything but on entering a council building and meeting the mayor has changed everything. We wait only 10 minutes before we are led through and asked, 'What do you need?'. 'Everything in your power you can provide for them' I say. It is broken conversation because I am translating from Spanish to English and vice versa. Over the next 40 minutes, the friendly but official mayor makes about 10 phone calls. Within this time, Maksym is registered in the area, he has a place in school, has an appointment to register there, we then go to sign up and collect his school bag before finding out he has Spanish classes starting every afternoon from today. As this all became apparent, Oksana breaks down in tears at the level of help she suddenly receives. It is an emotional

day especially when it all seems to come together so quickly after a few weeks of frustration. Maksym seems happy to be doing something. (Field notes, 'Maksym's lucky day')

This was one of the few lucky and fortunate experience the Ukrainians encountered because, as we were to learn, the mayor had been pivotal in making spaces available in the local school for the children. With regards to the Ukrainian women, however, in the absence of state support and formalised recognition of their work skills, viable job opportunities were only limited at best.

Online struggles lost to more pressing matters – Nastia

Even though Nastia had to wait to obtain Spanish ID which would permit her to work, she was keen to find some sort of job. Having experience of working as a basketball coach and even sports journalism, she took it upon herself to start applying for online jobs. Given that her Spanish was limited, she proceeded to look for contacts online. Within a week, she had applied for 14 different jobs before other issues started to interfere with her search. Her younger brother, Simon, aged just 16, already installed in another basketball scholarship in Madrid, suddenly lost his place in the academy because it went into 'administration', rendering him homeless. When Oksana and I looked into the detail of this, we found out that these two examples weren't isolated, and many sports institutions were turfing out young Ukrainians because of the additional insurance implications.

After a series of videocalls with her parents, and likely because she was the eldest sibling in the family, Nastia was charged with arranging Simon's asylum papers in Spain. In my flat, there was no room for Simon to stay so Nastia decided to leave with Masha and met their brother in Madrid before presenting themselves to the National Police as 'newly arrived' refugees – just as thousands of others had done whom we had seen just outside the police office. By doing it this way, they would be guaranteed immediate hotel accommodation while their papers were processed for an unforeseen amount of time. Even though Nastia and Masha had already presented their applications, the fact that they presented again in care of a minor would supposedly mean they could be fast-tracked. A week later, I went to meet them in the temporary hotel in a suburban area of Madrid not far from the airport:

> After looping off the M40 road, I follow another motorway which starts to head for the permanently sun-parched horizon. I pass row after row of industrial warehouses before following the tracking on the GPS to a side road which heads into a barren area harboured with far fewer. It is

here where I slow to a hotel which seems to be the mainstay for truckers heading across the country and stopping in the capital. The hotel looks odd against the industry as I get out of the car. Inside the reception area, the white minimal area is adorned with a water feature and a series of bored staff members dressed in grey and red. I wait in the reception area for Masha, Nastia and Simon. When they come down, Nastia and Masha bound up to me and hug me tightly. 'This is Simon' they say over each other as they pull off me as I gaze up at this 6-foot 6 giant. We shake hands as his light grip cripples my hand. Simon says, 'Hello Daniel, heard a lot about you'. 'You can see why he is good at basketball' says Nastia. They take me to see where they are sleeping in the hotel, but I get a clue after passing what seem to be sparsely-spaced rooms. When they come to theirs, we can barely get into the room before we are confronted with all three beds and an ensuite toilet. It is here that Nastia now dedicates 100 per cent her time on getting Simon into another basketball academy. 'I have an obligation to do this, I am the oldest, I am like his mum now' says Nastia as she shows me a list of possible avenues for Simon. 'This is him in action' she says as we crowd round her mobile phone to see a sort of compilation of his basketball plays. He has immense potential. (Field notes, 'Simon says')

Prestigious hope, false promises – Masha

Recognising the need to support her two younger siblings, Nastia gave up her search for work. While Masha learned Spanish through online teaching apps, Nastia looked for work opportunities within Masha's field as a pastry chef. The move to a hotel nearer Madrid meant that Masha was now on the doorstep of the capital, not far from good transport links to and from the centre. Within a few weeks of staying in the hotel Masha got a job interview at a restaurant in the city. After a few meetings with the owner, she got an offer of €1,200 a month, cash in hand, for four long 12-hour shifts per week. Even then, she said, this was a wage 30 per cent less than her colleagues were receiving in the restaurant because she was 'new to town' she was told. There was no mention of a contract and indeed she signed nothing on commencing work. The verbal offer did, however, have a condition attached to it, which was that she secure accommodation nearer the restaurant should she be required to cover additional shifts or if they needed to call her in unexpectedly. With high rental prices in central Madrid oscillating around €800–900 for shared accommodation, this meant that Masha would struggle to pay other bills like electricity, gas, water and food, let alone save money. Furthermore, if she moved closer, she would be obliged to start to pay other living costs and sign a minimum contract of stay with a landlord likely to be at least six months. However, to be able to get housing, she would need a work contract, which she did not have, so would therefore be unable to sign a tenancy agreement.

The other complication was that if she were to start working, she would forfeit her asylum application and void her access to housing support as she would be receiving a wage and be deemed self-sufficient (Chapter 1). Though now bunked up in a cramped hotel room, Masha was still keen to find work. Masha also said that even the hotel security guards were monitoring the times its clients left and returned to the hotel to ensure there was no identifiable pattern that may signify if anyone was employed or otherwise. She decided to take the risk, accepted the job and subsequently dodged the hotel security guards:

> The first few shifts in the restaurant were long and made more complex by the long walk from the nearest metro stop. After a few shifts in the restaurant, the security guards started to clock Masha's regular departures. When they asked her where she was going for such long periods of time, she said she was meeting friends and supporting them with their papers in other areas of Madrid. This seemed to be enough for them and no further questioning followed. The work, however, lasted less than one month because the long shifts took a toll on Masha's body. After one 16-hour shift, she returned to the hotel and the next day was unable to get out of bed due to the pain and fatigue. The 12-hour shifts she was initially promised were regularly surpassing 14 hours at a time and beyond that, at times, she was called in to do additional long shifts. Furthermore, the front room kitchen role she was also promised turned out to be a series of backroom tasks. The bonus payments to compensate the lower-than-average wage didn't materialise either. When she didn't turn up for work, three days later after the pain desisted, she was fired by the manager. (Field notes, 'Restaurant realities')

Between the nooks and crannies

Such struggles were commonplace among other Ukrainians looking for work and almost always related to precarious and unprotected work opportunities (see Chapter 1). By March 2023 – one year after the commencement of the conflict – only around 15 per cent of working-age Ukrainian refugees in Spain had found a job compared to an average of 40 per cent elsewhere in Europe.[2] And this was in the formal work sectors for it was often that Ukrainians found work in the informal equivalent. Informal labour markets are those where economic activities and employment relationships go unregulated by formal legal or regulatory frameworks. In essence, this segment of the economy operates outside official recognition, oversight and protection, and lacks the benefits and security associated with formal employment. Mitchell and Fazi summarise that:

> [O]ne of the most disruptive consequences of the global free trade architecture characteristic of neoliberal globalisation has been the emergence of a massive global reserve army of labour which, on one hand, has given multinational companies access to a seemingly unlimited supply of low-wage, highly exploited workers in developing countries, and, on the other, has become a lever for increasing the reserve army of labour and rate of exploitation in advanced countries as well.[3]

Given that almost all European countries are experiencing a decline in the working-age population – which undermines spending and leaves economies facing persistent shortfalls in demand – the current lack of aggregate spending is principally the result of structurally enforced policy decisions, not demography, namely wage stagnation and declining wage share caused by neoliberalism's 40-year assault on labour markets. As noted in Chapter 1, while the market continued to dominate the political horizon, companies scrambled to seek methods to retain high profits, labour laws were changed, and company policies were adjusted, thus creating the foundations for precarious work opportunities,[4] which some of these Ukrainian families were now seeking after leaving their home country.

Precarious working evolved quickly in Spain during the late 1990s and was accelerated by successive governments who were bent on shaping all domestic business and industry around global market ideologies.[5] The result saw a reduction in permanent contracts, increased precarious working opportunities and the expansion of informal labour markets. According to the International Labour Organization, currently around 25 per cent of foreign-born workers in Spain are surviving through informal employment[6] and this figure exceeds that of native-born workers. Immigrant workers are disproportionately represented in sectors with high levels of precarious work such as agriculture, construction, hospitality and domestic work. They are also more likely to have temporary or part-time contracts. For example, data from Eurostat indicates that about 30 per cent of non-EU immigrants in Spain are on temporary contracts, compared to approximately 20 per cent of native-born workers.[7] This is made possible because of the lack of full-time opportunities or legal work permits. Furthermore, there is a notable wage gap between immigrant and native workers. The Spanish National Institute of Statistics indicates that foreign-born workers earn, on average, 20–30 per cent less than their native counterparts,[8] mainly because the opportunity bracket they occupy consists of low-skilled, low-paid jobs. The low calibre of work also influences working conditions, so immigrant workers often endure longer working hours, lack of health and safety measures, and absence of formal employment benefits.[9]

Spanish host families – already working within an unforgiving neoliberal meritocratic system which heightens competition and responsibilises success as much as it does failure – had high and quick expectations that the new arrivals, irrespective of their backgrounds or traumatic experiences, would demonstrate the same dedication to the cause as they did and continue to do so (Chapter 1). Moreover, to some extent, they have also been ideologically charged to view new immigrants as problematic to the economy,[10] which douses them with meritocratic expectation to work themselves out of their newfound disadvantage.[11] It was therefore these deep schisms in the political economic system which were now felt and experienced in the growing everyday tensions between 'newly arrived Ukrainians' and Spanish host families.

Meanwhile, back in my hometown, with Maksym starting school, Oksana was able to resume her ad-hoc online consultancy work from Ukraine. However, one of the first women to get work in the town was Valentyna. As previously noted, in Ukraine, Valentyna had her own fashion shop and before the war had a good Ukrainian client base. With the advent of the war, however, she lost it all immediately. To her credit, none of this appeared to faze her or stop her from starting from scratch in another country where everything was unfamiliar to her, for, in the car with her and her family, were her two sewing machines. Valentyna's opportunity came about by luck really. As a gesture of goodwill, and perhaps to show appreciation for housing her mum with dementia and young Yesenia, she started to make her host family, Belén and Enrique, clothes. One day, in the local town, Belén had gone into a shop to buy more material for Valentyna when the shop owner commented on the very clothes she had designed and made. The shop owner looked on in awe, amazed at the quality of the cut and the flamboyance of the combination of the colours before telling Belén she would like to interview Valentyna for a job. The owner didn't speak Ukrainian and Valentyna had only a broken command of English which also didn't suffice. Belén instead asked me to facilitate the conversation, so I went to meet them both:

Shop owner: I am looking for someone to help out in the shop, help out with the sewing orders and generally help me clear the backlog. I had a young woman work for me, Spanish, but she lost interest and since then I have been running the business by myself.
[I translate this in English to Valentyna who tells me in her broken English:]

Work, study and cultural integration

Valentyna: No problem, yes of course I am interested. I have lots of experience, I had my own shop and ran global business. [I think carefully about how I translate this so it doesn't make the shop owner look potentially inferior – that they only run a small-town haberdashery. In the end, I tell the shop owner that Valentyna also similarly had a shop and a good client base.]

One of the main problems which evolved in the integration and assimilation of the Ukrainians in this small town was that often the Spanish host families automatically conceived of the refugees as people fleeing their country with next to nothing. This much was true. However, in that very same conception, they also framed them as people with no skills, citizens of poverty who were in need of charity and goodwill gestures. What is exemplary of this conversation, and later appears more apparent in this chapter, is how this perception defined the duties the hosts assigned to the Ukrainians as well as the gestures they made for them. It was this that was essentially rendering the 'refugees' the new 'undeserving poor' who seemingly could do nothing to help themselves and must only rely on the goodwill gestures of the hosts – no matter how tokenistic they were – thus sustaining a power imbalance. The conversation continued:

Shop owner: I want to help you, I will help you, I will give you some work. It is terrible what is happening in your country. I will give you a job. The work will mainly be fixing clothes and adjusting them. The hours will be 9am to 6pm, Monday to Friday and there may be some work at the weekend, but this depends on my clients' demands.
[As I translate this, I can kind of see the ideas start to flourish in Valentyna's head. While fixing clothes was something she had done in her early design years, it was not something she could be fussy about.]

Valentyna: Wow, amazing, that is fantastic! The hours I will take as I need to save money for my return to Ukraine, if it will happen sometime soon or even just sometime. What is wage, how much can I ask you pay me? Who will collect my children from the school?
[I then offer to collect Yesenia from the local school and translate this. The shop owner nods as if she has the moral high ground for providing the opportunity.]

Shop owner: The wage is €4.50 an hour [€4 below the minimum wage of €8.50] and I will pay you cash at the end of

	the week. I tend not to have lunch breaks because there is a lot of work so normally stop for 15 minutes or so. You can work from home as well, no need to come into the shop. Each evening, I will bring you the garments for you to tend to and collect them the following evening. [I communicate this to Valentyna who almost bursts with ideas.]
Valentyna:	You know, I could also make clothes for your customers, if they had special ideas or anything … I have this experience as well. [As I translate this, there seems to be a moment of interest and the shop owner's eyes make a seemingly judgmental look up and down at Valentyna's face.]
Shop owner:	No, this is not that kind of business. We fix clothes, we adjust garments. We are not a fashion shop [she says dismissively]! [I translate this as 'Unfortunately people don't contact us about fashion, just about fixing their garments.']

Valentyna sank back down into the chair at this point in the interview. Nevertheless, she still accepted the work. The irony of the agreement was, and I never had the heart to tell Valentyna, that whenever I passed the haberdashery shop thereafter, I never saw the shop owner working there during the day. It very much looked as if she had just simply subcontracted her work out to Valentyna. A similar situation occurred around the same time with Olena. Though she was quite shy and spoke no Spanish or English, Alicia managed to talk a friend of hers into giving her a small cash-in-hand job in one of the local hairdressers, cutting children's hair. I guessed this was the deal because elaborate designs or styles may have been more difficult to communicate without a better grasp of Spanish. The hairdresser shop owner normally charged around €5 per child for a haircut but told Olena she would only earn 50 per cent of that in cash: the hairdresser shop owner took the other 50 per cent as some sort of commission. Since she normally cut the hair of ten children each day, at best, Olena was earning around €25 and much of that time was sitting around waiting for the schools to finish since the owner insisted that she 'do her hours'. Unsurprisingly, quite quickly, Olena ran into disputes with the shop owner about the agreement and left within a week. Other Ukrainians, like Yana, ran into similar problems. Consider here how, like Valentyna and Olena, the presence of the Ukrainians, their skills or even just their ability to try and re-establish their lives generated a degree of insecurity and almost envy which borderlined on subtle resentment among some of the Spanish host families:

In the second week of May 2022, I start to receive some messages from Yana, a 30-year-old Ukrainian fitness instructor from the city of Херсон or Kherson as we have come to know through the news. The unfortunate geographic location of the city meant that, since the start of the war, it quickly fell under Russian occupation along with other key ports such as Маріуполь or Mariupol. It wasn't long before the Soviet Banner of Victory was flying by a WWII memorial in Kherson. Authorities in the Moscow-controlled Kherson Region announced only recently on 23rd May 2023 that the Russian Ruble would be introduced as an official currency alongside the Ukrainian Hryvnia.

I am not to learn this until I meet Yana who needs some help with registration for her resident's card here in Spain. Like Oksana, she contacted me through the same charity website. When I meet her in the neighbouring town of Boadilla Del Monte, her Spanish is minimal but her English slightly better. We are able communicate and between us navigate the frustratingly complex government websites to get her an appointment. Three months into the conflict and the bureaucratic systems seem to be working a bit better. But the ID is not her main problem it seems. She has had to move house after falling out with her host family and simultaneously losing her cash-in-hand job. When she first came to Spain in early March 2022, her host – also a single woman in her 30s – was accommodating and was even able to fix her up with a babysitting job, 7 days a week from 8am to 12pm. Her wage was just €4 per hour which was far below the average wage but Yana didn't complain. She came to Spain motivated and expected to be in such a situation. Instead, she tried to use the opportunity to generate some money to save and develop her fitness contacts. She even picked up a few clients quickly in the first few weeks.

However, when she started to make friendships, socialise, and was even invited on a date, the host seemed to start to get envious. Likely as a way of reminding her who was who, and who was where, and who had what, the host made references to Yana having 'nothing' while she, in tandem, had 'everything'. The relationship soured further when the host started bad mouthing Yana to her family and started to ostracise her. Shortly after, tensions reached a verbal stalemate, and the host then gave Yana three-days' notice to leave the flat. In a panic, she messaged me, but I had no rooms free. Through some people I knew, however, she was able to find some emergency accommodation the very same evening.

As she tells me this, she feels relieved: 'better to start again than be in that place, I was so uncomfortable plus I was spending a lot of money just to get to my job and wasn't earning much money at all'. Now she has guarantees that she has a room until the end of the summer while she builds her network. We convert her English CV to Spanish on my

> computer and I email it to her. I ask her if she wants to return to Ukraine. 'No, I won't go back, I have no life there now' she says. 'For one, I won't be able to return, it is Russian controlled' she adds. 'But your family are there' I comment. Her eyes well. 'Yes, but it is better for them. They speak Russian and it is better to be on one side or another, rather than in the middle, so they will stay' she says as her lips quiver. (Field notes, 'New contact Yana')

Like Kharkiv, the battle for Kherson started on 24 February 2022 but, unlike Kharkiv, the city was taken relatively quickly by the Russians. Because of its geographical significance close to the already occupied Crimea and the Dnieper River, Kherson was important to Putin. Residents in the city such as Yana's family described seeing multiple formats of Russian forces, tanks, aircraft and military vehicles surround the city. While 35,000 Russians took their posts to invade, only 500 civilians and the 192nd battalion of the Ukrainian Territorial Defences were to try to resist the inevitable occupation. Other brigades joined the effort but the Ukrainian losses were heavy and within four days the city had been taken. Ukrainian resistance efforts either abandoned the cause or died in the process. Humanitarian passages were eventually negotiated for those Ukrainians who wanted to leave the city while those opting to stay were asked to pledge allegiance to Russia.[12]

In the aftermath, it was reported that the entire Ukrainian Defence Force had been wiped out in Kherson, mass war graves were discovered and the remaining residents spoke of torture, detention and risked death if they showed opposition or confronted the Russians.[13] The surrounding infrastructure was so damaged, however, that basic resources became scarce and a humanitarian crisis ensued as the city's residents became ensnared in deprivations of essential commodities such as food and water. During all of this, Yana had continued to work in a gym in Kyiv but never contemplated a return to her home city. That door was firmly closed, that chapter of her life seemingly concluded. With her family confined to Kherson and expressing no motivation to leave, she reasoned she was unlikely to see them again and took the decision to leave the country alone. She hitched a lift along the already-heaving motorways of Ukraine and within a week was in Poland. She didn't want to present for asylum there because she had, in her own words, 'always dreamed of living in a hot country'. With no initial plans of leaving Ukraine, she now reasoned she may as well try and make that dream a reality.

Learning to suffer

With the unanticipated Ukrainian population in Brunete swelling at a fast rate, the mayor stepped up efforts in support of their cause. In the local newspaper there were glossy photos of the mayor alongside wealthy local business owners after meetings in which local companies were canvassed to generate manual work opportunities. The business owners, however, seemed instead content with the local kudos for the cause rather than actively contributing to it and no such openings evolved. With little success, the mayor then resorted to redirecting public works funds destined for a new playground (to fix the botched one mentioned in Chapter 2) into feeding more money into a private subcontracting firm called Greener Grass – the local company in charge of maintaining public spaces conveniently run by the mayor's brother-in-law. Just like the senior appointments made by members of the Ukrainian elite, neoliberal cronyism works on all levels, regardless of scale or location (Chapter 1). Known as *Jardinería* or 'gardening', the work was renowned for being both low-paid and physically demanding, which was probably why there were always vacancies. In the café, Valentin and Natasha recalled what happened, unable to avoid displaying their own neoliberal meritocratic expectation on their fellow country people:

Valentin: They [the Ukrainians] didn't expect that much money for a wage as they are much lower in Ukraine. There were so many different types. Some thought it was not enough money for the work, others, who had worse jobs, thought it was a lot.

Natasha: They were taking care of green areas, public spaces, cutting bushes, grass, weeding, etc.

Valentin: It was hot, 40 degrees, long days. They had to start work here, start at the bottom, suffer, like we did, all these illusions about how good Spain is or how good the work is start to disappear. That's when they start to other opportunities or reconsider life here.

Natasha: There isn't much. The gardening, or cleaning, or basic things. But no one stayed here so the temporary work was probably welcome as they didn't have any other direction.

Crude realities and childcare duties

This work was therefore a big reality check for the eight Ukrainian women who signed contracts – even without formal ID in some cases – with the local council's subcontracted company, Greener Grass. Generally, the women were required to tend to the upkeep of these areas so they were undertaking manual labour such as cutting, strimming, weeding, sweeping and the like. 'It is like we are working in a sauna all the time' said Anya after only her second shift. The Madrid province drifts very quickly from spring to summer and it is common that by May temperatures can reach 30 degrees centigrade. By June and into July the temperatures can reach 40 degrees centigrade. Most of these eight women thought it was proactive to accept what was pretty much the only work opportunity in town in the absence of knowing Spanish and with no recognised qualifications (that could translate to work in Spain). The grass, however, was all but green on the other side.

High expectations were placed on the women as they were given specific spatial targets to cover each day otherwise the subtle threat of a percentage wage docking was made. 'They tell us that if we don't finish an area, they don't pay us €10 from the day wage' Tanya told me. Rarely did they have breaks and didn't appear to have clear procedures around sickness or holiday. As I was to learn, the six-month temporary contracts they had signed meant that the employer was not obliged to cover them in the event of illness or holiday. Within a few weeks, the women were arriving home to their host families, wilting from the long hours working in the heat. Given that many of the Spanish host families drew the line at school drop-offs or pickups, the additional burden fell on a few people like me to collect the children from school and entertain them in the park until their mothers finished their shifts:

> Another early summer evening closes off as Anya finally returns from work. I have collected her children, Ighor and Milana, from school, taken them to collect Nadia, given them snacks and supervised their play in the park. Nadia and Milana lead the way [see Figure 4.2]. Zlata has joined them having been allowed out by Tanya. Ighor is playing football while Milana, Zlata and Nadia talk and play a clapping game from the top of the goals. Anya has not only been working in the fields nearby but has had to collect food from a local church charity which is open only two hours a week. She claimed she had other errands to run but I've since seen her drinking beer in another part of the park, seemingly disconnecting herself from the reality of her situation. She is a few hours late but compensates it by bringing me a beer. She offers me a cigarette, but I decline. Even though she has been here a few months now, Anya speaks no Spanish or English. Her work and children generally mean she can't make the free Spanish classes which run on a Wednesday. On the rare occasions she has gone, she has been tired and taken very little from them. There is a pressing need for her to save money as her flat has been destroyed in Kharkiv.
>
> Anya puts on a brave face for our selfie which she uploads to social media, then sits, sighs, opens the beer and lights another cigarette. She looks around as if she is still trying to catch up with her own life. At times, I catch her staring into space as all her thoughts just seem to draw a blank. I daren't ask her about her husband, a soldier who was killed early in the conflict, but ask her more generally how she is by putting my thumbs up and then thumbs down. We generally communicate through facial expressions

Figure 4.2: Nadia and Milana walking together, with arms around each other's shoulders

and gestures, mixed with the odd one word but on this occasion there are minute-long pauses as we type something out on Google Translate followed by nods in agreement. She types out a message while letting her cigarette hang from her mouth; the smoke all the time wafting relentlessly into her eyes which fail to surrender to a blink. She passes me the cracked mobile. It reads 'I am tired, I don't know what I am doing, and I want to go home. This life has nothing for me now'. Before I have a chance to respond, she looks up as there is a skirmish between Ighor and a local boy on the football pitch. Things escalate quickly as Ighor throws the punches fiercely at the other boy as a very sudden rage seems come over him; he pushes the other much taller kid to the ground before proceeding to continue with the punching. Anya seems unmoved and continues to smoke her cigarette and stares into space, so I go over and drag Ighor off the other kid. Play time is over. (Field notes, 'Play time')

Solidifying solidarity: Spanish classes and protest marches

After a series of brief meetings between Bea and the mayor, it was confirmed in our host WhatsApp group that the free Spanish classes for adults would commence on Wednesdays. Nearly three months into the experience and the classes seem to be the first step towards easing the integration. One hour will be offered to the children to complement their integration into school and another two-hour class will be for the adults. Bea asks another host called Maria and I to attend, along with Valentin and Natasha, to facilitate the communication with the new Spanish teacher. The night before the first class, however, and for the first time, some WhatsApp messages appear to concede to difficulties between the Spanish hosts and the Ukrainian families. Maria sends an unexpected and exasperated message about having some arguments with her Ukrainian family. There is little sense of what frustration is manifesting itself until Belén tries to quell it:

Belén: And I am sorry to say it, but although I know that it is difficult for us that we may find ourselves looking after a Ukrainian family with whom we do not get along, but at the same time it must be very difficult for them to leave their country and live on our charity.

Maria: For sure, it is a very hard situation and even if we can help them in all aspects, only they know what they are going through. ... I am sorry to say it too, because each person and their circumstances are different ... but some people also seem to take it as a right what they have, and that our hospitality is an obligation on our part ... and it is not like this. ... I think that all of us who have taken in these poor people have done it from our hearts, assuming it may change our lives and it may create some risks, but if living together becomes uphill, after we have tried to do everything for them, what do we do????? Just take it? And to live with tension in your own home????

The message seemed to suggest that there was a lack of reciprocity in Maria's house. In the words of Natasha, 'the Ukrainians don't like to ask favours but normally in Spain these sort of things come with the expectation of being repaid. The thing with the Ukrainians is there is no expectation to expect help back so this will have upset the Spanish as well'. This may have explained why Maria, among a few others, was starting to feel exasperated. There was a silence in the group and an hour passed before it was glossed over by Bea who tried to keep the general hosting morale high. The next day, however, Maria made an excuse and ducked out of the introductions at the first adult Spanish classes. As Bea was running late, it fell on my shoulders to meet the new Spanish teacher and explain how the sessions were to be delivered to the Ukrainians. I enlisted the help of Oksana to translate in Ukrainian for the women that didn't speak English. At 5.45pm, we walked down to the Cultural Centre where a roomful of Ukrainian women were waiting:

> Outside smartly stands David, the new Spanish teacher, who forthcomingly shakes my hand and introduces himself to Oksana and I. We walk in together on time but the room it seems is already full of Ukrainian women. Some sit slouched in their seats, others with notebooks, and a few on their mobile phone. David starts to talk and asks me to translate into English and for those women who don't understand rely on Oksana's broken English. As the three-way translation gets going, quite quickly around half of the women lose attention and get restless. I can't work out if this is because of the long working day or the genuine lack of interest in learning Spanish or even a combination. After the class, Oksana talks to a few women that remain before feeding back to David and I. We can only hope the take up will be high in the coming weeks. Oksana pulls me over to tell me Tanya made a comment about me: 'she say you are a nice owner' and smiles at me. Without even thinking what this may mean, I then try to explain to Oksana that I'm not her 'owner' nor do I 'own anyone' before Tanya interrupts by saying in broken English 'and she [pointing at Oksana] say you, you are a happy owner [pointing at me], yes, very happy owner'. (Field notes, 'Nice, happy owner')

At the time, I wondered if this forum would be the place which would unite the Ukrainian women together and solidify their integration, this alongside the work some were doing for Greener Grass in the *Jardinería*. What was clear was that efforts were being made to support their cause. The following weekend, Nadia and I were invited to protest marches alongside Nastia and Masha in the centre of Madrid, which were attended by thousands of people. The march not only gave the cause further regional profile but allowed the Ukrainians to expel the cacophony of emotions they felt about what was happening in their country, as well as keep alive outside political interest in their support. Nadia was certainly moved by what was happening and made a poster for the protests. In the car to and from the marches, she also requested the 2022 Eurovision hit 'Stefania' by the Kalush Orchestra. The song, which had been released in early March 2022, was initially written about the lead singer's mother, who was reminiscing about good memories of their relationship. With the Russian invasion of Ukraine, however, it had become a cultural motif of resistance and whenever it was played Oksana broke down in tears. Its popularity was such that it went on to win the Eurovision contest in early

May 2022. The supportive mood continued as Oksana and Maksym, Nastia, Masha and Simon, Nadia and I were formally invited to meet another host family at their home the following week by means of aiding the integration between the Ukrainians – at least this was the intention:

> I get a message from Alicia, another woman who has initially taken in a Ukrainian family of 11. We have been invited to their large house on the outskirts of town. We leave just after it has poured with rain and walk through the empty, puddle-sodden streets. We come to the property and stare in awe at the large house. Alicia greets us all with a hug and ushers us into her house. It transpires when we arrive that of the 11 Ukrainians, only four remain it seems as some have moved on to other properties. We all walk in – Oksana, Nastia, Masha, Simon, Maksym, and Nadia. In the doorway is a small woman with blonde hair also called Olena. She is 43. There is then her daughter, Katya who is 25, Artem who is 14 and Andrei who is 10. They all seem friendly and strike up conversations with my family apart from the two younger sons. Artem is shy and, according to Alicia, has barely spoken since his arrival from Ukraine while Andrei just wants to play video games all the time. In fact, as we try to introduce ourselves, he doesn't even look up from the screen.
>
> Oksana starts up a conversation with Olena and they hug as they seem to have a lot in common. I then meet Alicia's daughter, Rosa, and her husband, Alberto. Alberto is particularly vocal about the whole refugee situation when he says, 'the governments are doing nothing about these people, no help, no support, it is the people in Spain who are doing things for them ... if it wasn't for people like you and I they would be on the streets, there is just not enough state-funded accommodation for them'. When the family arrived a month ago, the town council didn't know what to do with them so Alicia and Bea went about trying to formalise avenues to be able to support newly arrived Ukrainians. (Field notes, 'New networks, early solidarity')

Even in March 2023, one year into the conflict, many of those Ukrainians who remained in Spain were *still waiting* for a €400 per month government grant which was supposed to support 'the most vulnerable Ukrainians':[14]

> Alicia welcomes us over to the table where she has made a nice spread of food and snacks, and Simon and I tuck in. After a while, Alicia beckons us upstairs to show us where the Ukrainians are staying. We walk up two flights of stairs to the roof of the house which has been converted into a mini-studio apartment. We walk in and there is an open space in the middle. To the right, there is an old sofa and another chair which sits opposite a TV. Behind that there is a double bed mattress on the floor and to the left,

behind another corner, is another double bed mattress. The two boys share one and the mother and daughter share the other. It is cosy but cramped and feels like a sort of decent squat.

We descend again and continue with the snacks and get to know our new friends. Suddenly, Alicia starts to bring out large bags full of clothes donated to her from other people – whom otherwise wouldn't have done unless she had told them about the fact she was housing Ukrainians. I follow her to where she fetches more bags before she shows me into the garage which is loaded to the ceiling with more bags. She starts to get all the clothes out and offer them to my Ukrainian family. It quickly becomes an odd and awkward situation because my family didn't think they were coming to her house to receive charity donations, but Alicia seems to insist. 'You have to take these clothes, you are refugees in our country, please take them' she says as my family start to reluctantly sort through the numerous bags. Olena looks on equally uncomfortable. As Nastia explained to me later, 'it was as if the tables had turned. In Ukraine, we were the ones donating clothes to the orphan children ... now we are on the other side receiving the donations. It is not a good feeling, and we don't want this kind of charity, we don't want people's sympathy'. After sorting and turning down suggestions from Alicia, Oksana and her family eventually make up a bag in the end, choosing clothes which will be suitable for the summer. They are reluctant to take more as 'other people will also need clothes so we just take what we need' says Masha. 'Believe me there are people with nothing so they need most help' says Nastia as she recalls conversations with Ukrainians, she knows who had sent her pictures of the piles of rubble which now represent their homes.

We start to leave and say goodbye, embracing them in the process. 'Please come by whenever you want' Alicia says to Oksana 'you are welcome to come here whenever, please'. While Oksana and Olena exchange numbers, the assembly of the two families doesn't seem to facilitate a natural urge to continue contact even if I think this is what Alicia was hoping. Indeed, at the next Spanish class, Olena is nowhere to be seen. (Field notes, 'New networks, early solidarity')

And Olena never did any of the subsequent Spanish classes either.

The Brunete Ukrainian Refugee Association?

I am asked to attend a meeting with only Bea and Alicia present. We share stories in the already stifling heat in Madrid and they reflect on some of the challenges they have with the families. One Ukrainian mother and daughter don't speak to each other because the daughter wanted to stay with her father in Ukraine. They've not said a word to each other in two months. Another boy in another family won't talk to anyone because he didn't want to leave his brother and father in Kyiv. And at the end of these troubling accounts of family difficulty, they announce they will be starting an Association for Ukrainians in town. They ask me to be the President but I'm not sure I'm qualified. (Field notes, 'President Briggs?')

By early summer 2022, Bea and Alicia, two of the most vociferous and dominant hosts and speakers at the meetings and cultural events, approached me to try and persuade me to lead a formalised association on behalf of the Ukrainians in Brunete. The mayor also summoned me to a meeting in an effort to convince me so the council, as well as the host families, could apparently access newly available central government funds. Curiously, as I was to find out in the small print, the president of the association (that is, me) couldn't financially benefit from proceeds. *Standard*, I thought to myself. But as president, I would be in collaborative control of funds which could be directed to Spanish host families (that is, Bea and Alicia). Things were moving at a quick pace for in yet another private meeting with Alicia and Bea a few days later, at which they seemed content to ply me with quite a few beers, they presented me with the paperwork and even offered me a pen so all I had to do was sign. I said I would read the contract and think about it. That very evening, the mayor sent me a series of WhatsApp messages essentially encouraging me to formalise all the paperwork before 20 June 2022 so the town hall could put on a local event celebrating Ukraine which would involve 'the refugees cooking for people in town' and 'lots of photos of us welcoming them' wrote the mayor. Anyone would think a local election was around the corner.

Notes
1. Duray-Parmentier (2023: 273).
2. OECD (2023).
3. Mitchell and Fazi (2017: 151).
4. Lloyd (2018).
5. Winlow et al (2015).
6. ILO (2021).
7. Eurostat (2023).
8. INE (2022).
9. Lloyd (2018).
10. Winlow et al (2017).
11. Briggs (2020).
12. BBC (2022).
13. Van Halm and Du (2022).
14. O'Mahony (2023).

5

Strained relations and trending 'solidarity'

In our host WhatsApp group, Bea summons all the host families to a meeting in early June and we sit down in the sweltering heat to hear her concerns. She is outraged to say the least when she says how Tanya – her Ukrainian guest, who is working nine hours a day, six days a week for a mere €700 a month – is not 'putting the money back into the house or contributing to bills'. 'Remember the government are giving us nothing for this', she adds. A few others who host women who work in the same demanding job nod their heads in agreement. 'It's like they are taking advantage of our goodwill and good faith', she adds, before criticising their efforts to learn the language, suggesting that she was under the impression that they would move on when they got work – even though she hadn't informed the family to work towards this. According to Alicia, one of the Ukrainian women in the working group is trying to persuade others to save money for when they return to Ukraine where many have no homes now. This was buttressed by further resentment, led by Bea, of how during the summer, the working women seemed quite content to leave their children at home – as they would have done in Ukraine when working during the summer holidays. 'And we are supposed to look after them?' asked Alicia.

This chapter charts how the initial sentiment of solidarity for these Ukrainian families quickly started to subside, leaving in its place a cancerous antipathy which was to form the foundations for more instability for the Ukrainian families. As discussed at some length in Chapter 1, neoliberalism erodes trust and unity, and has the capacity to damage and weaken collective solidarity because of the emphasis on individualism over communal welfare. This explains why the Spanish host families start to prioritise their own needs and desires over that of their Ukrainian guests as the initial collective mutual support networks dissipate.

Reshuffles

Valentin sits back in his chair and sighs before taking a sip of his drink:

Valentin: I don't know what happened with Anya and her family, they were kicked out by a Spanish family in a neighbouring town with a day's notice. Valentyna was looking with only

	two days' notice and she had to find somewhere. When Alicia and Bea found out about this, they wanted to know why she was kicked out but we were just looking for a solution. It was between all these people that we started to meet and we were involved in translations.
Natasha:	They were calling me more as my work is flexible, Valentin was busier than me.

Within a short space of time, the Ukrainian dynamics shifted as the teething issues associated with hosting, adaption and integration started to visibly manifest themselves. Anya, who was already working in *Jardinería* in Brunete, was given notice in her previous accommodation in Villanueva because, as she put it, 'I was working, they found out I had a job and expected me to pay them'. When she said she was saving for Ukraine, the family told her and her two children, Ighor and Milana, to find another place to stay. I was later to learn that what further soured relations between Anya and her previous host family was the fact that she refused to do any housework or contribute to the upkeep of the house – when there was a silent expectation to do so on behalf of the Spanish host families, which hadn't been communicated. Anya and the children were then given emergency housing with Belén and Enrique's neighbours, Ana and Fernando. It was Belén who managed to convince Ana to help them and, having seen how hospitable their neighbours were, Ana agreed; after all, two of her three children had left home and were studying and living elsewhere. Even though Fernando was reluctant, he caved under the pressure from both Ana and Belén. A day or so later, Anya, Ighor and Milana moved in.

Marina and her children had previously returned to Ukraine after only spending a month or so with Belén and Enrique. When Marina's husband left the family home and his job in Kharkiv and went to establish himself with other relatives on the western side of Ukraine in Lviv, Marina reconsidered everything. As soon as her husband got a job, the whole family returned – after all, reasoned Marina, they would be in a much safer part of the country and could return to their way of life with limited disruption. The children could return to school and familiar routines – even if, on the other side of the country, they were still at war with Russia. This new space in the house was filled by Valentyna, Yesenia and her mum. The fact that both host families (Belén and Enrique and Ana and Fernando) as well as both Ukrainian families (Anya and Valentyna and their children) knew each other aided the transition into the new modes of accommodation (see Figure 5.1).

Within the first week, both Anya and Valentyna seemed to settle in well and the fact that both host families had pets helped the children into their

Strained relations and trending 'solidarity'

Figure 5.1: Reshuffles (May 2022)

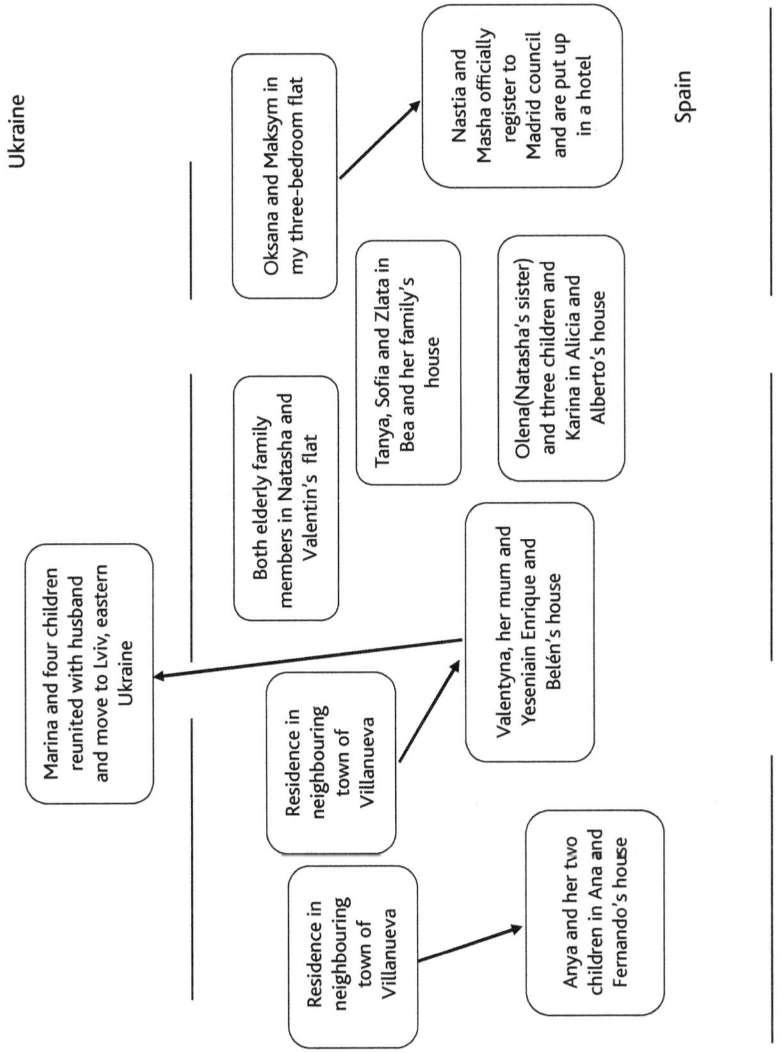

new life somewhere else once again. As we saw in the previous chapter, Valentyna was so appreciative that she started making clothes for Belén and took on the majority of the cooking for the whole household. Anya, conversely, seemed to sink quickly back into the same habits visible to the previous host family in Villanueva. Outside the long shifts in *Jardinería*, she spent long periods drinking alcohol alone in her room and left the children to find their own entertainment in the house or next door with Valentyna's young daughter, Yesenia.

Cultural events and mayoral attention

Even though these disagreements were surfacing between the Spanish hosts and Ukrainian families, the mayor sent me a series of voice messages asking me for ideas which could aid the Ukrainians' integration in town. With the school summer holidays imminent, the Cultural Centre would normally roll down its giant outdoor projector screen and shows films or series on Friday, Saturday and Sunday nights. Townsfolk over the summer months would attend and just watch from the park or the grass or even bring their own seats to the square. In my responses to the mayor, I suggested that there could be a *Ukrainian film night* or even, as an alternative, that *Servant of the People* be shown with Spanish subtitles. Given its brazen and overt discussion of political failures and corruption and having watched it myself with Oksana and her family, I thought it could be something to which the Spanish could relate. Jokingly, I wrote in a WhatsApp message 'it's like what happens in Spain but just on the Eastern bloc', referring to corruption and political ineptitude.

Only then I remembered that the mayor was a politician and there was then a long gap in our communication. Two days passed. Four days passed. The weekend passed. When I rekindled the idea the following week, the mayor replied within a few hours. The message read 'Thank you Daniel but what credibility does the council get from this?' Feeling frustrated that the council, in particular the mayor, simply wanted a popularity boost, I took to the host WhatsApp group with another idea: to show the Ukrainian World Cup qualifying game against Scotland on the same screen. In the group, Belén seemed to latch on to the idea:

Belén:	What a great idea! In the town's main café in the square, they always put football on.
Dan:	Which one?
Belén:	The one next to the monument.
Dan:	Ah right. I mean it's so the Ukrainians can get together, but also the Spanish love football, it is a universal means to get along with each other.

With some backing from the Spanish host families, I sent more messages to the mayor along the lines of 'the host families and I think it would be a great idea to show a Ukrainian football match'. The mayor, however, similarly seemed unmoved. *Perhaps it was the use of the screen*, I thought. The next day, I had yet another idea to hold a Ukrainian food festival in which the Ukrainians would make the food and the townspeople would come to sample it and make small donations. There was ample space in the main town square, overlooked by the mayor's office, so this could tick the symbolically-important-political-popularity box as well. All the proceeds, I suggested in another voice message, 'could go to the Ukrainians and the endeavours to repair their lives back home'. I concluded my final written message 'let me know soon so I can spread the word within the Ukrainian community'. Once again, there was a silence. A day passed, then two, and the weekend went by. I held back from messaging on a Monday but by Wednesday I reconvened the communication and received a response: 'It's not quite what we had in mind as the regional government have their own directive ideas', she wrote. *Then why ask me for ideas*, I thought, as none of them seemed to have been useful. I ran the new idea of a food festival by the host family WhatsApp group, which, aside from a few tokenistic emojis, only really seemed to capture the imagination of one person. The initial appetite to help and cultivate positive ideas to support the Ukrainian community seem to be falling on deaf ears with the Spanish host families, which was indicative of what was to follow. Yet again Belén was the only one to respond to my messages:

> Daniel, seems perfect to me, I think that creating links or activities in common is very important. And although for us this is just a challenge but it will always be more difficult, another country, other customs because we must not forget that many of them [the Ukrainians] have come having lost everything. We still have something. (Belén)

Two days later, I received a photo of a poster from the mayor and a request to pass it on within my WhatsApp networks. It was a campaign run by Brunete town council in collaboration with the Madrid government. When I opened the message and downloaded the poster, the crux of the campaign was not dissimilar to what Alicia had instigated herself – calling for the donation of clothes and non-perishable food, and stuff for kids. It felt like a campaign more directed at a developing country's needs rather than the immediate needs of a newly arrived Ukrainian community who didn't really want sympathy or to be treated as if they are 'poor and needy'. They all had their own clothes and instead preferred work stability or money to be able to save to return to Ukraine. Residents and citizens, the poster advertised, could donate at their local cultural centre.

I showed this to Oksana and explained that *Ucrania te necesita* – which dominated the poster – meant *Ukraine needs you* and she said sarcastically 'great, just what we need, more clothes and pity', recalling how 'it was like when we went to Alicia's house and she wanted to give us clothes!' I then shared it among the Spanish host family WhatsApp group where it received a couple of 'thumbs-up' emojis but nothing more. So Brunete town council stood in solidarity with the *plight* and *needs* of the Ukrainians. Those *needs*, however, weren't grounded in any kind of understanding of how Ukrainians were experiencing new life in Spain and bore no resemblance to the things they were concerned about, and the overflowing garage full of hand-me-downs in Alicia's garage was testament to this. All the messaging seemed to do was invoke a sense of impotence, rendering the Ukrainians 'helpless victims' and witnesses to their own lack of integration and bystanders to the public demise of their country – and this was certainly how many were being treated by their Spanish host families (see Chapter 4).

Meeting Belén and Enrique

By chance, Maksym and Nadia still have some energy to burn up after dinner, and when walking home from school earlier, we had seen some inflatable amusement activities for kids. Nadia badgers me to take her and Maksym down to have a go on them. Oksana seems preoccupied with videocalls to Ukraine and gives me the thumbs up to take them down. I grab some cash, some water and my keys. Even before we are at the inflatables, Maksym is bouncing excitedly down the road and Nadia chases after him until we start to see the first of the attractions. 'Palo loco' meaning 'mad/ crazy stick' seems to be what they are most drawn to. On they leap after I pay the gypsy owners who then seem to take a very relaxed attitude to what goes on – as in they sort of just wander off for a while and smoke cigarettes in the shade.

While Nadia and Maksym play on the 'palo loco', I overhear a conversation behind me between a local woman who seems to have engaged conversation with the gypsies who run the ride. They are talking about the Ukrainian families in town so I go over to introduce myself and we get talking. The woman I have quickly befriended is called Belén. She is one of the few Spanish host family members I have yet to meet as her work commitments interfere with attending the meetings. After the drama, she waves over her tired and weary-looking husband to meet me. Enrique shakes my hand strongly and embraces me as well. I feel like I am family already. 'The language issue is a problem' I say 'but with time hopefully they can start to find opportunities in the labour market' I add. 'Well, you have to be careful. We had one family with us for a month [Marina and family], and none of them worked, but we know other women in the area who are doing shitty jobs for nothing ... I mean long shifts lugging around heavy-duty stuff in the countryside for say €700 a month.' 'Wow, that doesn't sound good' I reply. 'It's exploitation but this local businessman is clearly benefitting plus also the government pay him for employing them so he is winning both ways!' Belén says in a disgusted tone. 'Oh dear. We were told by the local council there were jobs available in town but I didn't hear of these' I say. 'No, that's because this guy has got access to the Ukrainian family network and is trying to take advantage of their circumstances. It's all been done through the mayor. Our family have told us the women that come back after that work complain a lot about the hours, the fact they can't even go for a toilet break let alone a lunch break and are basically being exploited.' With that the gypsy woman blows her whistle to signal the end of the kids' fun. (Field notes, 'Chance meeting')

This was the first of many encounters I had with Belén and Enrique for, over the coming months, we were to continue to stand resolute in our support for our Ukrainian families. Meanwhile, the calls for more host family meetings gained more momentum as an additional preoccupation – mostly instigated by Bea and Alicia – was fanned out among the WhatsApp group. Another meeting was called for 'urgent discussions' as Bea wrote about 'pressing issues regarding the Ukrainians'. Now the concern was about our legal obligations as hosts. Just four days later this became apparent along with other additional issues such as the costs the Ukrainians were incurring to households:

There is then a head count around the table as we wait for a few more neighbours to attend the weekly meeting. I am introduced to a few more new neighbours who couldn't attend previous meetings before Alicia passes around details to register for government assistance. At the moment there is only a mediation service, no financial help, 'there is just a service which helps you with cultural differences but we already learnt we are different! It was the mayor who made the call to see which people in town could take families. Then when we started to receive Ukrainians, we went to the council but they said there was no money to help. Then the mayor passed our details to the government and some of the families just started to arrive' says Bea. 'But there is no legal insurance, like I say we are not legally covered for what we are doing' says Alicia. There is disagreement about how to register them with the government, as we share stories about getting their temporary Spanish identity cards. 'They don't want to deal with it [the government and local council], but it makes them look good' says Bea. There are then a series of preoccupations and complaints about the children staying at home before it turns into a general gripe about how the increased cost of food and electricity is now financially affecting the families. Belén, who I had only just met in person because she tends to work nightshifts, is the only host family representative who shakes her head in disagreement. Nevertheless, she keeps quiet. (Field notes, 'Urgent meeting number X')

Belén disagreed because she felt that, once we committed to such an endeavour as taking in a Ukrainian family, we had to see it through no matter what and that complaining about the challenges was generally unacceptable. 'Didn't anyone foresee these issues?' she wrote to me privately in a WhatsApp later that night. Initially, Belén and Enrique said in the WhatsApp group that they had 'done their bit' but when presented with a situation in which another host family was essentially making another Ukrainian family homeless, they stepped in and housed them. Valentyna, her mother and daughter, who had been residing with another host family in Villanueva and were evicted, were now to reside with Belén and Enrique. Belén was vociferous in the WhatsApp group, criticising the increasing trend of inflammatory messages against the Ukrainians and the hosts' general attitude towards the people they were supposed to be 'helping'. Shortly after, she got so tired of it that she left the group completely. I wrote to her privately asking why. She replied: 'Good evening Dan, thank God Valentyna is already in my house and not out there somewhere, homeless with her daughter and elderly mother. There are many attitudes that people have in that [Spanish host family Whatsapp] group that I don't agree with so I have decided to leave.' After her number appeared as 'left' in the WhatsApp group, the family responsible for kicking out Valentyna spoke up to alleviate the guilt they felt for the outcome while averting collective attention on them about the whole issue:

Well, now it's clear to me why Valentyna's abrupt decision to move to another family was taken. She told us on a Thursday night and yesterday (Friday) she left. … And I also believe that it is not a decision that can be taken overnight … even if it was a 'possibility'. Valentyna said she was going to go to Ukraine in July, to a friend's house who had offered her accommodation and a job. Finally, it could not be or didn't happen for some reason, so as we talked WITH HER, to find out if she was going to stay longer and if we should start looking for options in case she finally had to start making her life here … but also because in the following month's our situation could also change for several reasons. I mean the costs of things are increasing so much. We had been looking for premises for her so that she could have real chance of being a dressmaker – we even set up her sewing workshop in a room at home – and she was very excited about this possibility. We had also looked for a house where she could live and work with her mother, her daughter, we have also looked at the option of sharing a house with other families, talking with social services, with the council to see options to help all this ... and always with our support, that of our families and our friends. ... I think Valentyna has made a wrong decision and has been influenced by other people. The farewell has been very hard, for us and for them, because she is already part of our lives and we love them very much. She is a wonderful and very strong woman. Despite this turning point she will continue to be part of our lives and we will continue to help her in everything she needs. (Fiona)

After this explanation, there was an awkward silence which, after a few hours, was smoothed over by Alicia. The next day, it wasn't long before, once again, the Spanish host families start to moan again about the Ukrainians. That evening, however, I received a message from an unknown number at 11.42pm. It was Enrique, Belén's husband. 'We were speaking a while back outside the "palo loco", I am Enrique from the hosting Ukrainian families group', he wrote, before he quickly berated the other Spanish host families. 'It's a shame now that many of these people [Spanish host families] are talking about kicking out these Ukrainians from their houses, because of that, we have had to take in an extra family!' he wrote before saying they know another 'mother and children' in another nearby town who are also being kicked out (Anya, Ighor and Milana). The messages continued to appear in my WhatsApp chat: 'it looks like people are getting tired of "being nice" and are treating them like dogs, it's a real shame'. 'Its not right to kick them out for summer or give them an ultimatum but then consider them coming back in September ... .my wife left the group because the conversations were making her blood boil and she didn't want to say something to offend anyone', he noted, before describing how 'in the same host group was Ana, who also had to take in this extra family who were kicked out from another town [Anya, Ighor and Milana], down the road, and they are really wonderful people'. 'Anyway, its getting late, come round for some beers so we can talk about it', he finished.

As the weekend approached, the frequency of Enrique's messaging increased and Nadia and I were invited over for some food and a few drinks. Aside from seeing them, we would also be meeting their son Adrian, who had various learning difficulties and mental health issues (ADHD, Tourette's and autism) and their 13-year-old daughter, Grace:

> Though Oksana is invited to Enrique's, she declines as she wants to focus on Maksym's outdoor basketball practice. It takes Nadia and I only eight minutes to walk there as they live just past the school where Maksym now attends. As Nadia and I walk on to their road, we encounter a tall, spacious four-bedroom house which is part of a closed, gated community. I buzz the doorbell and Enrique opens and embraces me with a beer in his hand. Past him run Milana and Ighor who immediately hug Nadia and they all run inside to play together. As I go through, I am greeted by a huge dog which leaves on me its gunky saliva, 'Don't worry about the dog, it won't bite, it will dribble though' he laughs merrily. I am shown through into the living room and around the house, all the while distracted by an amazing smell coming from the kitchen. 'Do you want a beer, come on you have to have a beer?' he says with a huge grin on his face. When I say yes, he hugs me tight. 'Come through this way' he says as we walk through into the kitchen. There working hard at various kitchen stations is Valentyna; she is cooking *Kotlecky* (meatballs) and pulls me a seat. 'Try one, please it is my honour' she says as Enrique brings me a fresh cold beer. Then in comes Enrique's son, Adrian, who is excited to meet me; he bounces up and down and nods his head back and forth. 'Do you play basketball, we can play together' he says. 'Adrian, go play, we need to talk' Enrique says to him before he turns to me. 'Where do we start with these other Spanish families?' he says as he cracks open the drink, 'They are an embarrassment to humanity, they care more about themselves than the Ukrainians they are supposed to be helping'. (Field notes, 'New neighbours')

Here Enrique makes a stinging critique of the brittle support network, which is perhaps aptly reflective of Hall and Winlow's extensive work on the hollowing out of social community relations (see also Chapter 1). In much of their work over the last decade,[1] they chart how the decline of traditional social structures and collective identities in contemporary society, particularly under neoliberal capitalism, have resulted in the weakening of collective social bonds and mutual support for other people – much like what Enrique lamented over the course of this evening. Much like we learned from Chapter 4, the Ukrainians' struggles in the labour market and here their difficulties 'integrating' into Spanish are compromised by a meritocratic moralism of what is expected of them coupled with individualistic preferences to prioritise themselves over their guests.

I sat and drank with Enrique and Belén, and I got to know my new acquaintances as Valentyna continually brought out an endless supply of

Ukrainian delicacies for us to try. Enrique was an unemployed teacher who had spent the last five years telling himself he needed to take updated teaching courses to be able to return to work. He lost his job when his alcohol use got out of control after separating from, and then divorcing, Belén. The separation lasted only six months, however, as they got back together mainly because of their son, Adrian, who was suffering in the absence of their support. Belén was a nurse but had the weekend off after working six nights in a row; she certainly seemed to be very quickly relaxing as she too drank more beers. It was easy to feel comfortable among them as the alcohol flowed. After Valentyna finished the cooking, she went to coax Anya out of her room to join us to drink. For Anya, however, drinking alcohol had become second nature, not that her hosts Ana or Fernando knew too much about this in the beginning.

Ukrainian parties

Over the next few weeks, Nadia and I met Enrique and Belén, their families and the Ukrainians on several occasions during the town's summer festivities. While I tried to maintain some contact with a diminishing group of host families, my friendship instead grew with Enrique and Belén in the wake of their ostracisation by the other host families. Nadia, too, became closer to both Ighor and Milana, which aided in the general adhesive nature of our new relationship. During one evening in the town's main square and between chasing after Adrian who seemed to risk potential conflict with the local young people as he randomly hugged groups of women, Enrique swung his heavy arm around me and said philosophically 'I already questioned the humanity humans actually have but now there is no need to question it, this whole experience with the Ukrainians confirms it'. It felt like Enrique could no longer disavow his own accumulated cynicism of the world,[2] for he was almost transfixed on the failure of the whole operation. Every time I saw him, he came out with the same stinging comments about the flailing commitment of the Spanish host families. As we drank late into the night once again, his dissatisfaction at how Spanish host families had treated Ukrainian families just became louder and louder, to the point that his remarks were almost echoing around the square. A week later, Nadia and I were invited to another party at Enrique and Belén's house where we were to learn that Ana's household might receive yet another Ukrainian family:

> The party is lively when Nadia and I arrive, the drinks are being shared around and the music blares out and echoes around the quiet neighbourhood. No Ukrainian delicacies tonight, just instant junk food as oven pizzas and crisps are laid out as well as an array of beers. Enrique

has set up a projector screen onto which, as the drinks are sunk in high spirits, are put a series of music videos. Perhaps as expected, *Stefania* by the Kalush Orchestra is put on and the Ukrainians embrace, sing and cry as they watch the video. It's difficult not to hold back the tears particularly when Valentyna explains how the key word of the song is 'колискова' – which means '*lullaby*'. The word returns in both the chorus and the verse, as each rap verse ends with the sentence '*Lyuli lyuli lyuli*', which Valentyna explains is a classic Slavic folk lullaby. The sound of the lullaby, she says, brings them back to a moment when they were still under the safeguard of their mother – likely symbolising for them a desire to return to pre-invasion life in Ukraine (even if it was corrupt and bereft of political direction).

Then, and by my complete surprise, Tanya and her two daughters Sofia and Zlata arrive. They have come from Bea's house where they have stayed since arriving in Spain. They are given drinks and then Zlata goes off to play with Nadia, Milana and Ighor while Sofia sits in the corner on her mobile texting her new Spanish boyfriend. Tanya, who is a lot more standoffish than Valentyna and Anya, shakes my hand and produces a wry smile before sitting down. We all start talking though it is difficult to hold the conversation as Valentyna and Anya randomly come over to hug me and encourage me to drink more. When things quiet down after the music volume is reduced because of complaints from the neighbours, I get chatting to Tanya. It turns out she has been told to leave Bea's house before the summer and hasn't got a place to stay; she hasn't even had the heart to tell the children yet. I tell her I would offer my spare bedroom but it is still used by Oksana and Maksym. Enrique gatecrashes the conversation and tells Tanya, 'Don't worry, that's why we invite you today, Ana, come over, come speak to Tanya' he bellows. Ana comes over with her beer in her hand. 'We wanted you to know that if you need to you can stay in our loft' and as she says yes, tears rapidly roll down Tanya's face and the steely-cold demeanour which is commonly hers evaporates as she throws her arms around Ana. 'Thank you, really, thank you so much'. (Field notes, 'Party')

The cost for living versus the cost of living

> The longer the hosting period lasts, the more the host is confronted with a new reality: he/she is no longer alone in his/her private home and the desire to return to his/her old habits and homeostasis becomes more and more felt. He or she may then be caught in an inner conflict of welcoming and wanting the guest to leave.[3]

Here, Duray-Parmentier describes how the 'reality of hosting' dawns on the host, and how the initial hospitality dissolves into welcoming yet simultaneously wanting to move on. In the context of this study, however, these cultural and spatial divergences were aggravated by wider shifts in the wider global political economy which had implications for Spain's national economic performance, providing further evidence of how market logic debases social solidarity.[4] Figures released by the National Statistics Institute (NSI) in June 2022 indicated that inflation in Spain had increased by an additional 1.5 percentage points, bringing the overall rate to 10.2 per cent: the highest level recorded since April 1985. Higher prices in the consumer price index, the NSI concluded, were related to the higher costs of food and energy, which had a knock-on effect on the price of hotels, cafés and restaurants. The main reason, the NSI concluded, was because of disruptions to global supply chains initially during the COVID-19 pandemic but thereafter further aggravated since Russia's invasion of Ukraine.[5]

Added to the bubbling strains between Spanish host families and the Ukrainians were then a sudden raft of cost-of-living pressures, such as a negative impact on household consumption, increasing uncertainty, unpredictable stock swings, supply chain disruptions, bulging utility bills, decreased investment due to political risks, and economic growth impediments.[6] Quite quickly things started to look gloomier for the Spanish host families as the cost of living quickly started to dent the hosting rationale, particularly since many, such as myself, were housing the Ukrainians for free. Many in fact, as we will see, were in reality unprepared to spend more to keep others in their homes if it meant sacrificing their comforts such as their holidays. Instead, the increased costs further stoked up conversations about the perceived lack of appreciation among the Ukrainians and the perceived lack of interest they showed in 'contributing' to the increasing household running costs, even though some of them had exploitative, low-paid jobs. The *cost for living* (and supporting) the Ukrainians had been superseded by *the cost of living* for the host families.

All of this gathered momentum very quickly, for as June started to close, Bea summoned all the Spanish host families to an emergency meeting. Yet only half of the host families attended as we sat down in the sweltering heat to hear her concerns. Interestingly, what Bea didn't reveal was how she had given notice to Tanya and her family to leave, and instead launched into a tirade about them – perhaps in preparation to tell us that they were 'leaving of their own accord'. Bea spoke indignantly when she informed us of how Tanya was not 'putting the money back into the house or contributing to bills', perhaps reflecting elements of her self-sufficient, entrepreneurial spirit and business mindset (Chapter 1).[7] 'Remember the government are giving us nothing for this', she added. A few others who were hosting women who worked in the same demanding jobs, nodded their heads in agreement. 'It's like they are taking advantage of our goodwill and good faith', she continued, before criticising their efforts to learn the language, suggesting that she was under the impression that they would move on from her accommodation when they got jobs. Alicia chimed in with similar comments and told everyone about how one of the Ukrainian women in the working group was 'convincing others to save money for when they return to Ukraine' where, even if the majority had no homes left in Ukraine. Further indignation was then later shared in the host WhatsApp group:

> I think some of these Ukrainian women have got it all wrong about our hosting. They consider it something owed to them on our behalf and a right because their country went to war. They are not even capable of putting themselves in our situation and the reality is we are very tired of it all. It is affecting our family relations, our finances and because of it we won't be able to go on holiday this year. (Alicia)

What a situation: favouring a holiday over the continued help for a family who would otherwise be homeless I thought to myself. A week later, I learned that another Ukrainian family from the town had returned home to Ukraine. For reasons related to childcare, Gloria informed us that she didn't want her Ukrainian family to stay for the summer and left the next meeting. Belén, Bea, Ana, Alicia and I had tried to find alternative accommodation for the family but had found no solution. In the WhatsApp group, it was then formally announced by Gloria before she abruptly left the chat. There was then a very long group silence.

Mutating moralism and strained relations

The pattern by which moralism was directed onto the Ukrainians may have only been publicly shared by predominantly by Bea and Alicia, but others too shared the same feelings, as I found out in private conversations with some of the other Spanish host family members. By now, there were heavily strained relations between almost all the Spanish host families and the remaining Ukrainians, confirmed in these two field note sequences. Some days later, I bumped into Gloria talking to a friend in the café:

> As I greet Gloria, I seem to interrupt a moaning soliloquy about the Ukrainian family she had hosted. It seems that Gloria had told the family that they could have short-term accommodation but would need to find something by September. The main disruptors for Gloria were the additional household costs and the differences in ways of cohabiting.

> 'I mean if they are working, why don't they rent out a place together? Two-bedroom flat could host two families for example' she reasons. The Ukrainian families seem to have a plan she thinks but staying and living and working in Spain doesn't seem to feature according to Gloria who summarises that there have been 'poor government integration efforts'. It's perhaps easier to blame a larger entity for its failure to grapple with the issue of refugees and their integration than to reason with oneself that they may have failed in their own helping venture. (Field notes, 'Gloria's reflection')

Here the disavowal permits Gloria to alleviate responsibility and emotionally disconnect from the consequences of her decisions and actions. In a café opposite, only the next day, I pre-empted the opportunity to talk to Roberto, another host family member I had met through the meetings and cultural events. I invited him for a beer to discuss things in more detail:

> 'One has to adapt' demands Roberto as we sit with some beers before the meeting. 'I can't tell them what to do as I am not their parent' he reflects. 'The 16-year-old doesn't even talk to us, there is tension between her and the mum, she wanted to stay with the father, she wanted to leave.' He continues 'then there is the day to day, I would have thought they could do their own ironing but the mum, has the cheek to say, "Well don't you have someone once a week to clean and iron?" I mean she does the garden work, in the fields, she earns money.' He goes on to say how he feels invisible in his own house. 'There has to be mutual respect', he says firmly, 'but there is none on their part'. I ask if they have looked to rent. He says no. 'Rent is high around here, the prices have gone up' he says as he shakes his head 'and in general landlords ask for a year contract when these people are living day to day, monitoring the situation in Ukraine'. (Field notes, 'Roberto registers his complaint')

Roberto is conceived by his Ukrainian family as economically superior as he can afford a cleaner once a week who tends to the communal areas in which they stay. Yet the suggestion that they – the Ukrainians – could also benefit from this resource is overruled because Roberto can only configure their presence around *the things they should be doing for themselves or the contributions they should be making to the household*. As June ended, the moaning continued about the increasing cost of living, how funding could be sought to support the Ukrainians, where they could live, and how they could be more independent. To add to the situation, the Spanish host families that remained start to be 'concerned' about what the Ukrainians would do with their children over the summer, while some of the former left for their holidays:

> There is furore among the Spanish host families. They are up in arms about what childcare will take place over the summer. After speaking with Oksana, Anya and Valentyna, it seems that the cultural attitude to childcare in Ukraine is to just leave children at home while the parents work. In Spain, however, it is the opposite. Normally children are put into summer camps if they have no parent or guardian at home. Even if the law is quite ambiguous about it, the cultural expectancy is that children will be cared for by an adult. The local town hall don't seem to have thought about this support (yet) so instead there is talk about how the families will pay for them even when, in the words of Bea, 'they are earning money so they could enrol their own children in the schemes'. Others chip in with similar indignant comments before Natasha, who has hardly attended any of the host meetings, speaks up for the Ukrainians. 'I am not sure you really understand, most of these people', says Natasha, 'most of them have completely lost their houses, lost their jobs, livelihoods, in some cases, lost their husbands or men they know and they have nothing' she appeals. 'They are saving now, whatever they earn, they are keeping for rebuilding their lives' she adds. 'Well, we aren't paying!' says Bea as the majority nod in agreement. (Field notes, 'Summer dilemma')

Perhaps unsurprisingly Natasha refused to attend further meetings and, with that, the translation help and mediation that she had been providing abruptly ended. The Spanish host family meeting attendance was by now so limp because the hosts had just lost interest in the issue of Ukraine or their family had moved out to try their luck somewhere else or returned to Ukraine. By the beginning of July, interest was renewed in the idea of persuading the remaining families to live together in a large residence. Rosa wrote in the host WhatsApp group:

> I am writing to inform you that my husband and I are starting to look at rentals in the area for our Ukrainian family so they can move forward in their integration. I think it is necessary, since I think we are all aware that unfortunately, the situation in Ukraine is not changing. For a single family, it is a bit expensive now with the increased prices, but for 2 or 3 families it can be viable. Social services told me that if they manage to establish a rent, the Ukrainian families involved could apply for help, for a couple of months, and there are usually no problems because they have minors in their care ... they say a few families have already done it in neighbouring areas of Madrid

with other Ukrainians. Not sure how successful it has been though. I don't know what situation you are all in but thought I would let you all know. (Rosa)

Rosa avoided most of the previous rhetoric around the cost of living and made a pledge to the remaining host families around the notion that integration must take place – even if, for most of these families, there had rarely been a permanent commitment to Spanish life or living long-term in Spain. Bea was quick to reply to the messages in the group when she wrote how 'by September they should be independent, living with each other' but that she couldn't understand why 'Ukrainians don't want to live with their compatriots ☹'. The collective buckling of support continued to stoop to new lows when, within a matter of days, another host family announced that they had taken steps to shed their household of Ukrainians. Writing one afternoon mid-July, Lorena informed us that:

I have a meeting with Social Services next week and I am already talking to them about the possibilities so my [Ukrainian family] can plan what they decide to do from now on. I am quite disconcerted with the situation and right now I feel that a line is being crossed in our house and I feel uncomfortable about this. I think that once you have a job, you have to take a step forward towards independence and I have not seen my Ukrainian household do this so, for this reason, I am asking them to make alternative plans. (Lorena)

No doubt that some Spanish host families had encountered difficulties with the Ukrainians but all the rhetoric from Bea and Alicia now seemed to be resonating with almost everyone else in the group, and in the case of Lorena, stimulating then stoking the very concerns she seemed to have had all along. Follow-up messages joined the same moralistic carousel from the moderators of such conversations, Bea and Alicia:

Bea: We can support them from networks separate to ours, they should be independent as soon as possible.
[Less than 30 minutes later:]
Rosa: I understand this but, at the same time, it is a necessary step. At least for me the goal is the insertion into society until they can leave: [As they say in Spain] not to give them fish but give them the rod to learn how to fish.
Alicia: That is also my goal.
Ana: Mine too, but it seems a little early given the uncertainty in which they find themselves, the situation they have lived and continue to live. I, for my part, have offered to take them in

for an unlimited period of time. If this is not your case, you could talk about the possibility of changing families.

Trending solidarity

Ana, and her husband Fernando, were one of the few remaining host families who took such a stance, along with Enrique and Belén and, perhaps less obviously, myself as I made no real public comment to anyone or any side or any perspective. The quick disintegration of community solidarity in the face of increasing costs and cultural differences combined with the souring relationships between the hosts and Ukrainians are evidence of a neoliberal condition that has reduced us to think only of ourselves in times of collective adversity. The strong emphasis now placed on personal success, self-reliance, and individual achievement and reward prioritises personal interests/goals over communal or societal responsibilities (Chapter 1). The brittle commitment to helping the Ukrainians in these examples typifies our pervasive culture of individualism, evident in the Spanish host families' words and actions as they rotated towards the protection of their own needs, ambitions and consumerist desires over their willingness to commit to helping others. As we saw in Gloria's reasoning, such a position inevitably inverts the possibility for self-reflection and self-analysis and pushes out attribution on to other external factors:

> They are also influenced by their leader [Tanya] and in my house she has created several conflicts. For me, it is important the existence of this group, it has already been demonstrated that they are united and we, as good Spaniards, are not. And we need to be united to at least support each other and dismantle the hoaxes and lies that are transmitted among them. I feel we are a failure as a group. They are going to have the wrong feeling, that is to say that we are going to continue giving them everything by right and it will complicate our lives. I think they should be more autonomous. For our part, we have not seen many changes in that sense of autonomy so we have to set deadlines to ask them to leave. (Bea)

Also palpable in the experiences was the increased cost of living and, in some cases, mounting debt. These pressures seemed to make many of the Spanish host families more focused on their financial status and less inclined to invest time, energy or resources into helping the Ukrainians. Then, only a few days later in the host family WhatsApp group, Rosa joined the growing rank of people leaving the cause:

> I have already talked to our Ukrainian family to tell them that we are going to look for a house for them during the summer. It is unrealistic

for us to be able to continue to support them for free. It has been very difficult for me and I do not feel good at all because it is a new setback for her and I do not know how she is going to deal with it (I am only telling you all this this to get it off my chest, it is a hard pill to swallow). I am writing to see if you know anyone who can stay with her and the two children (a 13-year-old girl and a 12-year-old boy). The family are very nice and the relations seem good. Tomorrow I will talk to the Council to see if they know someone who can accommodate them and someone said about the Town Forum, but I do not know how this works. Thank you all! (Rosa)

And with that, yet another Ukrainian family left their hosts. We all want to believe and commit to a cause just like we all want to believe and commit to a solution, don't we? Or is it more that we want *to say* we commit to a cause? I say this because the 'help' many of these host families offered seemed to have been well meaning at the outset but after some time the realities of co-habiting started to reveal the cultural schisms and social expectancies. In some cases, it felt less about the cause and more like about how the Spanish hosts used the experience as an indicator of social status, to appear 'good' and *as if* they were doing their bit for the cause. Throughout this whole experience, some of the Spanish host families – as well as the mayor – were regularly publicising their charitable efforts on social media channels. This can be argued to raise awareness about the issue and be a potential mobilisation for the 'cause'. On the other hand, however, as Thimsen[8] would suggest, such actions represent 'performative activism' where *the activism is done to increase one's social capital rather than because of one's devotion to a cause.* The rapid disintegration of 'actually supporting the cause' represented instead a superficial sense of engagement, where liking, sharing or commenting on a post is mistaken for genuine action (Chapter 1).

Even though the mediascape compellingly flooded the channels with live updates about the evolving war between Russia and Ukraine, it quickly became a 'trending cause'. Our emotive attachment to help a 'trending cause', coupled with the brittle commitment to see it through, represents a 'trending solidarity' and evidence provided in this chapter illustrates how it can dissolve quickly into bitter feeling:

Valentin:	Then in the background there was all this media reporting of it, the poor Ukrainians, the bad Russians, people trying to escape the country, the pictures of the children on TV, the bombs. It was flooded into many media channels, in many languages, in many different countries. It was done to get people to feel something for it, like in an emotional way.
Natasha:	But it was like a changing fashion. Something comes into fashion, and you buy it, then something else comes in

fashion and you forget that and buy the new thing. It was like that with the Ukrainians: people felt like they should help but they got bored and tired of it.

Notes
1. Winlow et al (2015); Winlow and Hall (2022).
2. Winlow and Hall (2022).
3. Duray-Parmentier (2023: 273).
4. Winlow and Hall (2022).
5. National Statistics Institute (2022).
6. Mbah and Wasum (2022); Ozili (2022).
7. Fazi and Mitchell (2017).
8. Thimsen (2022).

6

Pastures new and war sirens old

Within six months, the solidarity and willingness to help the Ukrainian families was quickly wilting away as the higher cost of commodities started to affect the Spanish host families and many grew impatient for them to be self-sufficient. Additional resentment had even crept into a few households when two of the women employed in the exploitative manual labour sectors had got additional cash-in-hand jobs and were earning more than the Spanish host family households, thus negatively disturbing the ideological meritocratic pecking order. Nastia and Masha, perhaps foreseeing rifts and the limitations of the economy and opportunity in Spain, decided to leave the country completely: Nastia took up a job in Italy working remotely as a basketball reporter and Masha returned to Poland to stay with a friend before making periodic and risky trips to see her parents in Kyiv.

Olena and her children were asked to leave Alicia and Alberto's house and left for Germany. Bea, in particular – who had told everyone she was instead receiving a Syrian refugee family – was almost emotionless when she offloaded Tanya, Zlata and Sofia onto Belén and Enrique. As we saw in the last chapter, when they received Tanya and her daughters, they were not only housing Valentyna, her mother and Yesenia, but also their own children, Adrian and Grace. Increased capacity in the houses, particularly Belén and Enrique and Ana and Fernando, added to increased tensions. In my case, I regularly found myself looking after the children – Ighor, Milana and Yesenia, along with Maksym and my own daughter – during the summer holidays as their Ukrainian mothers continued to work. While the war showed little sign of diminishing, one by one, the remaining families returned home and this was exacerbated by the conclusion of the temporary work contracts for any extension would mean employers would have to contribute to social security payments and employees would be entitled to sick pay and holiday pay, among other statutory rights.

Crisis of solidarity in the Eurozone

Beyond Brunete and the Spanish borders, similar patterns of solidarity weariness and help lethargy were observed. As the Ukrainian/Russian conflict continued, the initial wave of support waned, giving way to growing fatigue and logistical challenges. The prolonged crisis strained resources and infrastructure in many European host countries, leading to concerns about housing shortages, job competition and the financial burden on social services. In response, some European nations began to implement stricter immigration controls and border checks, reflecting a shift from initial openness to more cautious and controlled acceptance. The sentiment towards Ukrainian refugees also shifted, with instances of xenophobia and anti-immigrant rhetoric becoming more visible in some regions. Political parties and groups leveraging nationalist and populist agendas began to capitalise on these sentiments, framing the refugee influx as a 'threat to national identity' and 'economic stability'. This shift in public opinion and political discourse influenced government policies, resulting in more restrictive measures and a rejection of Ukrainian refugees.[1]

All this shifted collective public sentiment and this was most poignantly reflected in Poland, Europe's largest receiver of Ukrainian refugees. Research conducted by the Research Laboratory of the University of Warsaw and the Economic and Humanitarian Academy in Warsaw during the summer of 2023 on Polish public perception of Ukrainian refugees and migrants found that support for assistance to Ukrainians among Poles significantly decreased. A quarter of Poles were reported to have said 'no' to additional aid for Ukraine. Moreover, the percentage of those strongly supporting assistance to refugees in Poland fell from 49 per cent in January 2023 to 28 per cent in May 2023.[2] In the latest Protection Monitoring Report in Poland published in September 2023 by the International Rescue Committee, it was estimated that over half (55 per cent) of Ukrainian survey participants had experienced at least one form of labour market discrimination and that just over a third (35 per cent) of Ukrainian respondents had experienced tensions within their Polish hosts.[3]

No country for young women (or their children) – Alicia and Bea

Late in 2023, 18 months after the experience, I meet again with Alicia and Bea who I had not seen for some time since the Ukrainian exodus from Brunete. They join me in a café after a Red Cross workshop and I order them a couple of coffees. From Tanya and her two daughters Sofia and Zlata, 'I get sent a photo or something here or there', says Bea, while Alicia tells me that Olena has no contact with her. Quite traumatically for Tanya, Sofia, her teenage daughter, insisted on staying in Spain with her new boyfriend and they now live together somewhere in Madrid. Zlata, her youngest daughter, returned to Kharkiv with Tanya. During the conversation, it transpires that Bea had absorbed all sorts of unintended challenges and invisible issues[4] (see Chapter 3) when receiving Tanya and her family; many of which she hadn't shared during the host family meetings but which shed much more light on the complex dynamics in her household. She explained:

Bea:	One of the many problems I had was that Tanya had no relationship with Sofia, her 17-year-old daughter. Sofia lived with her father when Tanya separated from him so when the war started she had to leave with her mum with whom she has not spoken for years. There were arguments and fights. Sofia disappeared for five days while she was here in Spain. Many of the conflicts came from how she [Tanya] had brought up her children and the relationship she had with them. In Spain, you can't be five days without knowing where a minor is. Tanya wanted to go home but no one wanted to assume responsibility with a minor … it was crazy!
Alicia:	They came with them their family problems from Ukraine. And there were families coming which weren't together or had these sorts of problems.
Bea:	Put on top of that the fact she was an adolescent, changing and growing and rebelling.

They then proceeded to say how Katya, Olena's eldest daughter, was 'practically the mum' because, in Alicia's view, 'Olena didn't really care that much about the children'. Things seemed to be going quite well, Bea thought:

> We did everything for them. We helped them look for work, we got them the papers, we fed them, we supported them as we could. They took a lot of money with them, they saved it, they took it, a new experience and went back healthy. She didn't think much about the children. She just wanted protection. Look, they left for Germany where they got protection but the kids had already made friends, were in school [in Spain], learning the language [Spanish], they were settling well but then they had another change. (Bea)

Alicia then tries to put a positive spin on the experience by adding how 'some good things happened' because 'in Ukraine, Katya and Karina's relationship would have been seen badly but in Spain this is much more accepted'. But the possible advantages are quickly quashed again as they both seem to recall the problems with the Ukrainians. In another example, Alicia reveals how before she came, Olena had said nothing about how her ex-partner had been living in Fuenlabrada, another poor district south of Madrid. 'One day he suddenly turned up outside the house and we didn't know who he was or if he was violent or anything, we knew nothing about the terms of her separation or on what grounds they wanted to see each other' says Alicia. Then there was the potential 'negative influence' the Ukrainian children were thought to have had on their children:

Bea: I have three children, nine, 11 and 14. We always sit down to eat *together*, I get them to eat healthily, vegetables, etc, and it's the only time of the day we are together. We always eat together to be able to talk and share things that have happened. So, we have the Ukrainians at the table, the youngest one we serve with broccoli, but she pushes the plate aside, reaches for the bread and puts ketchup on it. And my children were shocked. She said 'I don't like vegetables'. So it's like we put them up but were asking to at least respect these things, the way we do things or want to do things. Then after I call them [the Ukrainians] to dinner but they don't come and it's just everyone does it how they want. We have our dinner then they have theirs. So, from there we just started separating. We have a calendar where twice a week, one adult cooks with a child and we do it so they can learn to cook. They didn't do that which is fine but they didn't want to respect that we did it like that.

Alicia: I learnt a lot and committed some errors. There was a language barrier, cultural differences. You hope and expect that if people are coming to live with you and find a better life that they would learn things in the new place which could help them live their own lives there. I think if you try to insist, you have a worse time. It's a lost battle. Take the issue of what happened with cleaning the clothes. They were in the attic but never used the washing machine. I go up one day wondering why they haven't put the washing on and Olena has handwashed all the clothes and they are drying in the room and causing damp and humidity. All the walls badly damaged. 'Look, there is the washing machine', I said, 'please use it', but she never brought her clothes down to wash. They had no intention of learning from us, adapting or looking for a new life.

Bea: I think living together is what is most difficult. Tanya wanted to leave her children at home all summer and there were free summer camps but she didn't want them to go. If there is a problem in my home, what do I do, who is responsible because she is working.

Alicia: They came with a mindset of 'all-inclusive hotel'. I make the dinner for everyone, them included, I make Alberto's dinner first as he eats early and then wait for them to come down. Sometimes I was waiting until 11pm for them to come down to eat!

Bea: We looked for things in common but couldn't find it so we just let them live their lives. We didn't want to let them lose their cultural things but what can you say. You can't involve yourself in how they do things.

The reflections continued as Bea comments on how many of the Ukrainian family tensions and struggles spilled over into the everyday dynamics of her own family:

> The time when the girl [Sofia] disappeared for five days and Tanya had no real reaction, this was the worst, this was when I thought they had to go. I get up at 7am to wake the kids up and I find her and a young man sleeping in the living room on the sofa. So, I say to the guy 'What are you doing here?' and he says 'It was getting late so I decided to sleep here with Sofia'. It's like, what the hell is this? I said to Tanya, 'Talk to your daughter' and she said she doesn't talk to her so it was up to me so I said 'You can't do things like that in our living room' so a few nights later after she had started sleeping in the attic, another different guy comes back with her! My children are seeing this and thinking they can bring anyone home and I don't want this for my kids. But the other thing is legally I am responsible because she is in my house but Tanya doesn't care at all because of their poor relationship. I don't know who she has been with, where, if he is aggressive, if they used condoms. I came home another time and there were their clothes and underwear strewn all over the living room, in the bathroom, and she was with a different guy! (Bea)

They then remonstrated about how they lobbied the mayor for funds for summer camps but in the end none of the children went and how it was, according to Alicia, 'a total embarrassment'. In hindsight, and fitting for the neoliberal scenery which governs subjective thought systems, they treat the experience as *something which enriched their lives as individuals* rather than being *something for the greater societal or collective good*,[5] all summarised by Bea as she describes how it helped her children learn 'about the different cultures, what they do, what is the right thing'. Without wanting to formally give them notice, they used the Spanish social care system to try and relocate Tanya and her children with little success:

Alicia: We had official visits, they [members of the state] came and made an evaluation – and this was after three months of us taking them in – so the only thing I wanted to be assured of is that they would be reverted to an official system or programme of support. When they finally came to make the evaluation, it was a disaster, it must have looked totally abnormal. The Ukrainians were so tense, maybe because they thought it was some sort of evaluation of if they deserved to be in Spain, they were quiet, they were tense, they said nothing, nothing to reassure the evaluators that we were helping them. But the main problem was they had come to us first instead of presented themselves to the system when they arrived so the doors were already closed.

Bea: They didn't want to rent together, the Ukrainians. So, there are problems with the host families so you would think that in this situation they would want to be together but they didn't. We got the kids into school, fought to find them work opportunities, tried to engage them with Spanish life but they didn't want to help themselves as a group much. Zlata, Tanya's youngest daughter, was very complicated. The school director tried everything, nothing worked. She wasn't interested. She didn't want to talk or be with anyone. Andre, another Ukrainian, used to play with her, but she then started making excuses to avoid school. Illness or whatever, in the end she didn't really go. I just felt they didn't try enough at things.

Speeding but all fine – Yana

Well, there were other Ukrainians 'trying' only they too weren't having much success. Once again, Yana messages me asking for more support. This time it is about accommodation as she had been evicted from another shared flat. As Oksana and Maksym had left, I agreed to take her in and postponed my intentions to sell. I collected Yana and brought her over so she could unpack her things. I was to be the fourth person to host her since she came two years into the conflict:

> It is Yana's second day staying in my flat and even though she is owed money, she has none to make her travel. I offer to take her to Boadilla Del Monte where one of the few remaining fitness clients she has still contracts her hourly services. Time is short as I will lose time out of the working day to deliver and collect her. During a break between my meetings, we briskly walk down to the car. I am keen to return as soon as possible to make my next meeting. In the car, I take the turns quickly and pass a police patrol car which pulls me over. Thinking I may hopefully get off with a telling off, I talk apologetically to the policeman and explain the situation. 'You think you are the exception just because you have a Ukrainian to help?' he asks before saying 'everyone has an excuse'.

He studies my driving licence and doesn't seem to understand why the steering wheel of the car is on the opposite side. He walks off, radios a colleague to check my driving licence and ID as I tap my fingers on the wheel. 'That will be €150 because of the speed you are doing, you were 20km over the limit' he says. He hands me the ticket and I drive off slowly. Yana just looks out of the window and says nothing. I break the silence to ease the tension, 'Its OK, it could have happened any day' I reason this thinking that of course I would not normally be doing these speeds. Perhaps the worst of all was that when Yana gets to her class, her client can only pay her €50 of the money she is owed. Today was definitely a loss all round. (Field notes, 'All fine')

Holding out – Karina and Katya

After leaving Brunete because of the limited work opportunities, over the summer of 2022 Katya (Natasha's niece and Olena's daughter), moved in with Karina in a small, shared flat in Colonia Jardín, a deprived neighbourhood in the southwest of Madrid. 'Shared flat' in reality means they share a room and the flat is shared with other people. Two other Colombians occupied the other room but relations were fairly distant as Karina recalls, 'We don't normally talk much, they also work long hours. The guy is a fast-food cook and the girl is a waitress', reflecting the reality of life for people working in precarious and saturated urban industries in the neoliberal era (Chapter 1). The rent they collectively pay is €1,000 a month which is split between the four of them so Karina and Katya must find €500 a month to cover things. While all the bills are included in this rate, food and travel costs are additional. Any extra goes back to Ukraine: 'Sometimes I send money home, can't really save much, just about getting by each month. Between us, some months, we donate to an army charity which organises food and utilities for soldiers' families as prices are high in Ukraine.' (Karina).

Note how they commit the little extra they make to their country and the war cause, perhaps still believing in victory. While Karina seemed to pick up some dental assistant work quite quickly, largely because of the general 'sympathy for Ukrainians', as she puts it, Katya had to wait a month before she was successful. She even managed to find two jobs: one cleaning in a suburban hotel and another as a waitress in Boadilla Del Monte. In the café as we talk, Karina now speaks a little Spanish and her skills are slowly advancing, perhaps because of her academic background. Katya, however, still struggles with basic words in Spanish and often finds herself making hand gestures or relying on Google Translate. For the first six months of being in Colonia Jardín, Karina was completely reliant on Katya's wage:

Dan:	Has it been easy to get work?
Karina:	No, and this is my second job in a surgery. I didn't have job so I was months looking, sending out messages, emails, CVs. One then contacted me for an interview in January 2023, six months I worked there. Then in August there were problems because they didn't want to pay my holidays so I looked for another one. They said they would start to pay again in September with a new contract. In this second company, the boss says he wants to convert my qualifications. [Sounding doubtful] We'll see.
Katya:	I work 20 hours in one job and 20 in another.
Dan:	Do you think the wage is good?
Katya:	My last job was better paid than these two but this is the first time I am doing two jobs but I am not sure how much I will get. I don't understand the wage systems. I don't like my jobs at all now. I work because I need money, need food, pay bills but I am looking for a job that I like. I can't work in an office because I really don't speak the language well.
Dan:	What do you not like about your work?
Katya:	I work six days a week, one free day. It is hard work. Long hours. It gets me down, I have no direction.
Dan:	Do you want to stay in Spain?
Katya:	Yes, for now.
Dan:	What is your plan?
Katya:	It's really important to learn the language, for communication to work otherwise, it is no good. I want to study a course in university but this is a long way off.

Before arriving in Spain from Kyiv, Karina had just finished her dentistry degree and had started work in a practice as an assistant and, just before the war, had been promoted. Katya, meanwhile, was working as a receptionist. Now, having been in Spain for some time, they not only find themselves still struggling to get work related to their skillset but also to get fair pay and equal recognition – hallmarks of life in our neoliberal wonderland of infinite opportunity and where hard work is the only answer to relieve disadvantage (Chapter 1). As part of a 'immigrant precariat',[6] they are subject to overt discrimination and institutional blockages within the workplace:

> In the first company, I was the worst paid employee. I got the least out of everyone. Cleaning staff were paid better. It was in Moncloa [a rich district of central Madrid]. I started at 7.30am in the morning, little money, lots of hours. I had a contract but it was paying me less than the minimum wage in Spain. Normally, with the more time you

work, the wage goes up but my wage never improved. I spoke to a colleague who said that I should have the minimum wage but I had less for some reason. (Karina)

Karina spoke several times to the manager and was made promises but saw no change in the conditions or wage. Katya, meanwhile, was currently being paid in cash in hand at restaurant which was, by comparison, 'less because I am Ukrainian and I don't understand how things work but I do, but then again, what can I do? It was like that, even in my first job here'. Katya had already exhausted many different work opportunities but found it difficult to hold down work. Here, she reflects on her short time working in a neighbouring school as a cook. Even then, the pay she received was less than her contemporaries and she ran into difficulties with other workers:

> I had some conflict with a woman who I was working in the school canteen. We were in the kitchen, this woman, a cook, thought she was really important, she had been there for years, and I was the new girl in town who didn't know how things worked and didn't speak very well so she was always angry with me, shouting at me. (Katya)

The kitchen job Katya undertook followed the work she did with her mum, Olena, in the *Jardinería* which abruptly ended when the contracts weren't renewed to avoid the employer's obligation of offering them secure work. 'Then I was cleaning houses, paid in cash, for five or six months, but the money was like so bad, like €5 an hour', she said. By the time she had started working in the school, she had already been through four different jobs. Yet both are adamant that staying in Spain will reap the benefits with time and persistent hard work – proof that they have assimilated and absorbed the neoliberal expectation of themselves that Valentin described eloquently in Chapter 1. And with war still raging in Ukraine, the most they can do is work to live and take intermittent risks to return to see their family:

> I went back to see my mum, grandparents and I hadn't seen them for 18 months. I took a plane to Poland (3.5 hours), then a bus (10 hours), then a train (24 hours). I went myself in the end. I have no fear, it is like normal now. They live there and it's like a routine, the bombs, the war. I was a month in Kharkiv, there were fewer bombs but you still heard the noises. In some places, there are unexploded bombs, people just walking past. The whole thing is completely normalised now. [Karina gets her mobile out and shows me photos and videos she took from her local neighbourhood.] Inside these buildings around

where I live, it is more dangerous so no one goes in, no one lives there now. This block, for example, had 400 people living there, most left as it was unsafe after the bombing but some stayed as they have very little money and nowhere else to go. (Karina)

She struggles to fight back the tears when she says that her grandparents are 'too old to leave, imagine for them this is the third war they see in their lives'. Katya's mum, Olena, along with her two brothers, left Spain because of conflicts between the host family, Alicia and Alberto, and there was no work for them. Her circumstances in Germany, though, didn't seem to have improved because, like millions of others trying to survive in similar unforgiving circumstances around Europe,[7] she had simply slotted into equivalent grey areas of the German economy:

Katya: My mum found it difficult here, to live here with the people, she didn't find work, the mentality of the Spanish. In Germany she has family, she has a brother there.
Dan: But why didn't you go there first?
Katya: She want to see her sister first [Natasha], to make it work here but it didn't. Mum is now working as a hairdresser at home, she is helping out with an elderly person. It is not official work, cash in hand. The economy is bad in Germany and there is a lot of control on people coming in so it is quite strict. I wouldn't like to live there. I went there in September to see mum and my brothers as it had been one year! It was a happy time but then I had to come back to reality. In Germany, they are under a programme and have to complete stages as part of the integration contract, they have to learn the language and my brothers are doing this but my mum is bad at languages so I am not sure what will happen.

There is no promised land, no golden ticket and, by cruel paradox, the grass is certainly not greener on the other side, it is just grass. But their futures, at least for the time being, are committed to making it work in Spain, even if it has been challenging (see Figure 6.1 for a summary):

I don't want to go back to Ukraine. It is better here. The language is difficult but I prefer it here. The first year here was difficult, there is my home, bit by bit it has been a bit easier and I feel different. The only problem is my work and career. I don't know what my future is here but there is no future in Ukraine, I think what I would do if I went back. At least I can work here. I do miss my home though. (Karina)

Figure 6.1: Autumn change (September 2022)

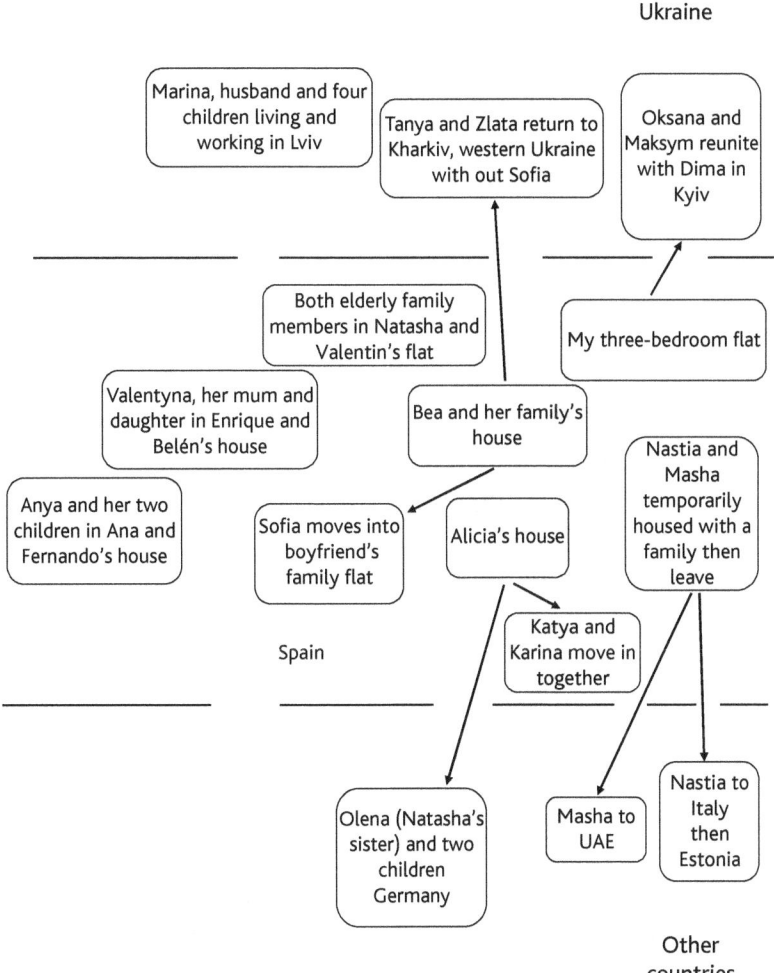

Pastures new

After waiting months for the asylum system to determine where Nastia, Masha and Simon collected their ID at the end of September and, in late October 2022, they were finally moved back to Boadilla Del Monte, my neighbouring town, to be housed with another Spanish family while their request for housing was put on a long list. Like with numerous references they made to the potential move, it was another opportunity to mention where their real home was:

> Our home is in Kyiv! But we have to make do with these homes for the time being. We have been matched with a Spanish family and this

family is almost the same that we have. There are five kids and we are out of four. Two of them don't live in the house which is why there is room for us. Both are three storey houses and they even have the same dog 🐶! (Nastia)

There, they were to wait until appropriate accommodation could become free, once again sharing the space with another host family. Nastia recalled their hesitation, mainly because it meant more moving and no guarantee of long-term housing, not that she made this reservation clear when accepting to move in:

It is just a first seven days try out, it has all been done through the Red Cross. Tomorrow will come social worker to resign documents concerning our living in this family. Everything seems good by both sides so we just could stay here next six months. I have managed now to pick up some online spots work last week and have now started Spanish courses online, this was always the delay because I had to prioritise Simon and Masha … but during the general relocation I did this. We are here now for the first seven days are like try-out so hopefully we won't have to move again! (Nastia)

The timeline wasn't that clear but they were told to expect to be there for around six months by which time they were expected to enrol in Spanish classes and start to be independent. Deciding that it was perhaps safer to move in and rely on the hospitality of another family while they decided which best steps to take, they were surprised to see that within a week they had received a visit from a social services representative to discuss the social and spatial conditions of the house. The visit made them feel increasingly unwelcome and that the Spanish state mistrusted them in some way. While the host family were clearly warm and friendly, things that they had heard about from other Ukrainian settlers started to become a reality when tensions increased about living arrangements and contributions towards house tasks and, suddenly, it had the prospect of becoming the same experience for them as many of their Brunete contemporaries (Chapter 5).

Meanwhile, with the advent of the new academic term, I invited Masha and Nastia to give a presentation to my Victimology class at university. Even after asking the whole class to attend out of courtesy, only ten of 25 came, but that is another story attached to the unmotivated privilege with which many of my former Spanish students went to university. On the day of the presentation, Masha and Nastia came in with a PowerPoint presentation filled with photos of their life pre-conflict and testimonies of what happened when Russia invaded. I'd like to think those students left with something but in truth it was Masha and Nastia who seemed most grateful to be able to share their experiences about it.

The day after their appearance at the university (see Figure 6.2), however, I received a message from Nastia asking me if I had any contacts in Estonia. Puzzled, I replied asking why only to be told that Masha had been offered a job with accommodation in a restaurant in Italy and that, while they went there, Nastia was going to apply for job she had seen advertised in the capital, Tallinn. I called a friend I know in the city and asked her to provide support to Nastia who, by all accounts, had already bought her ticket but had no accommodation. 'We have to leave here, Daniel, we are out of options in Spain, there is not stability and the people here not understand the Ukrainian way of life' she wrote. Nastia had tried to arrange some accommodation in Tallinn but was told that 'owners don't want to give Ukrainians freebies'. After the successful online interview and unperturbed by the uncertainty, Nastia left her sister in Rome, and boarded her flight. 'I know that the centre of refugees is in the main bus station and they could provide hotel' she wrote to me with some confidence. She at least had a job even though she had nothing else, perhaps indicative that these are increasingly the attitudes and personal requisites with which people need to equip themselves as they begin the eternal battle of survival among an expanding mass of people locked out of formal systems of support and opportunity (Chapter 1).

This all happened on 29 November 2022. On 30 November, Nastia presented herself to the refugee centre to a 'woman who speak Russian perfectly' and was set up on a national database and put up in a hotel. 'I tell them I won't need long for support as I have a job and show them email

Figure 6.2: Nastia and Masha delivering a class

offer so they agree to give me hotel a few days' she wrote. By 2 December, Nastia had signed her work contract. That very same day she had been to the police station to present her documents for a National ID card. Two days later she had 'found good flat to rent', which had a 'separate kitchen, room with bed and a bathroom, small but a place', she wrote, adding how it was 'not far from work in an Estonian speaking district'. She was even more amazed that she had this for just €320. The main problem was that the flat was empty, 'no dishes, no cups, no pots, no pans, no kettle, no pillows, no blanket, nothing', so she called my friend the next day who brought her some old unwanted house products.

Over the next few days, and with the help of an advance payment from her new workplace, Nastia was able to buy the remaining things to make her new flat her new home. During the next two weeks, she embarked on numerous training programmes to adjust to the new IT demands and, shortly after, even had the capital to pay for Masha to visit her. As Christmas neared, however, they realised it was potentially to be the first without their parents who were still in Kyiv. Nevertheless, Masha planned a surprise visit to see them 23 December and, and with the advent of the new year, Masha wrote how 'the bombing was loud over Christmas but I am happy to be at home with my parents'. Nothing can describe, wrote Nastia, the 'happiness they had for seeing her, their children' even if it 'is risk, we think the worse that can happen is that there is no electricity for communication', she wrote, adding:

> Me and Masha needed to do something, we were going nowhere in Spain and start from the very beginning in new countries. Tough as it was, I feel better we did this. I am working in a good company, I am productive, I am contributing to something, I feel like I am active again and it feels more like emigration life, not as a refugee! (Nastia)

War sirens old

By late autumn and early winter of 2022, the fragmentation was almost complete in Brunete. If the Ukrainian families hadn't left, they were pretty much feeling the pressure to do so. In September 2022, Oksana and Maksym also decided to return to Kyiv, citing an easing in the fighting as an opportunity to alleviate the feelings of missing Dima and other family. Continuous contact with Oksana and her family became difficult thereafter. The power outages and unpredictable raids meant that only periodic messages could be exchanged. On 5 October 2022, she wrote to me that she couldn't even go shopping 'without the air alarm starting'. Each time, with each warning, Oksana and the citizens of Kyiv were expected to head underground as soon as possible. My messages and voice notes were met with prolonged silences. It took ten days for her to tell me how 'we don't have electricity, so there are problems with the internet. Due to massive infrastructure strikes in Ukraine, there are problems with these things now 🤷‍♀️'.

It was difficult to maintain contact or even, when asked how we were, feel comfortable about making reference to our relative safety. Nearly two months passed, and my WhatsApp messages remained unanswered until early December when Oksana wrote again to say 'I am well as I can be in the absence of light, water and heat☺. Today again another rocket attack and problems with light, heat and internet☺'. The Christmas period approached and my messaging continued but with little response until early January 2023:

> Everything is complicated. Constant air raids and rocket attacks disrupt normal life. In addition, there are problems with electricity and the Internet. Winter was good for us this year. It's not very cold. During the day -3, at night -7 or -12. A few days at the beginning of January it was even +10. This is very unusual. But the problem is that the frosts lead to a lack of electricity, due to the infrastructure destroyed by Russia. (Oksana)

Meanwhile, in Brunete, contact between Spanish host families all but subsided after the mass exodus from the town until, late in 2022, Enrique humbly wrote an early new year's reflection in the WhatsApp group:

> After hosting the 1st Ukrainian family [Marina and her family], we had the option of hosting a 2nd family, who were invited by their host family to leave their home as soon as possible. We have been very happy with this [second] Ukrainian family since the summer, that we left them our house when we went on vacation, that they have taken great care of us, and then we have been living very well together since August. My Ukrainian family will remain here for now until they can return, when the war is over, or the situation and area is recovered and normalised. Courage, peace and perseverance to all! ☺✊✊🙏 (Enrique)

With the advent of 2023, I called in to see Enrique. Walking in, Adrian called out 'What's your surname, Daniel? What's your surname?' 'Briggs' I told him as the dog escaped the door and jumped up at me. The place was quiet, organised and clean. Not like how it was earlier in year when the house was full of Ukrainians. Belén was not only working nightshifts but now overtime, necessary with the increased costs of commodities, higher bills and the steep rise in mortgage interest rates. Enrique came through and embraced me before beginning his hunt for beer in the fridge. 'The idea to host was through Belén, who is quite religious, when it happened, she said we have to help in this war and it was the best way to help to take them in' he said as he moves cheese and milk and reaches to the back of the fridge where the coolest part of the fridge stored the beers ice cold. As we sat and opened our beers, he said with some irony how 'Anya was friendly but a bit mad, an alcoholic really although she wouldn't admit it!' Contact had quickly become patchy with both Valentyna and Anya, who both retuned to Ukraine at the end of 2022. He talked in a fashion between lamenting and reminiscing, and as always, was still highly critical of the 'help' many of his fellow country people had offered when the conflict arose between Russia and Ukraine:

> Valentyna was with the typical Spanish family who are not prepared to take people into their house, when I say that not even to stay for a night. If you are someone who has infinite love for your home, your house, keep it tidy, don't like children touching things or using things, why would you invite a family with children into your home? You see lots of Spanish people are like that. Why foreigners? You don't even know them. They are not even from our culture. They thought that we were more advanced than them but maybe it's the other way around! The kind of people that get surprised that in their home countries they have televisions and [shakes his head] … I mean the funny thing is they thought they were European like them, and from an inclusive point of view, that may be the case, but these cultures vary a lot even within Europe. (Enrique)

Critical of a globalised vision and an increasingly homogenised culture, Enrique said how, in the end, the 'whole one culture sounds beautiful but it is full with problems' because 'people have more differences than similarities' (see Chapter 1). Smiling fondly while he recalled the memories, Enrique remembered how Marina, who stayed with them for just over a month, spent half of that in Ukraine. He nudged me as he finishes his first beer and says:

> You know that she left her four children here, went back to see if she could smuggle her husband out of Ukraine, she was away for two weeks, trying to work a way out of the country but in the end she thought if she did this, they would not be allowed back. (Enrique)

Enrique then returns to the fridge for more beer. Some of the differences Enrique said were related to how Ukrainian women 'delegate motherhood', as he described it, because he remembered how Marina 'had her eldest caring for the baby and the nine-year-old looking after the four-year-old' even if 'sometimes there were arguments with eldest and Marina'. As it was, the family reasoned they couldn't continue without being together so Marina returned to Ukraine with all the children. When Valentyna came during the early summer of 2022, his house filled once again with new guests. He admired Valentyna's work ethic – even if it was exploited by the locals:

Enrique: Valentyna was working a lot of hours in the shop here in Brunete.
Dan: Right. How did it work?
Enrique: They split everything down the middle, 50 per cent. It was an elderly woman but then she wanted to pass the running costs of the shop down to her so that was 50 per cent. It was costing €600 a month to run the shop so before Valentyna has taken home any money, she has €300 taken from her. But she was working from home, here she had her machine and when the shop wasn't open at the weekends, she was working extra hours here. She was earning €750 a month so that minus the €300 was €450 which is a bit over €100 a week for a full-time job.
Belén: I said to Valentyna it wasn't even worth it.
Dan: Anya used to come down to the park sometimes and then leave me with Valentyna's daughter, Yesenia, plus her two, Ighor and Milana, and I was with Nadia and she would ask me to look after them
Enrique: Not really worth it and look what happened with the care of the kids.

As he opened some nibbles to mix with the cold beers, he added:

> Valentyna, well there no need to talk to her about contributions, she was always doing things, buying food, cleaning, cooking for herself and for us but we never asked money for electricity or anything like that. You can see that from a young age she was independent and determined. Not like Anya so it wasn't a surprise when she had her crisis, that Ana and Fernando asked her to leave. (Enrique)

Anya's crisis

Anya's 'crisis' may have been something inevitably waiting to happen. Much like the previous Spanish host family that had received her, Ana and Fernando were also expecting Anya to contribute to house chores or at least socialise somewhat. 'She was in her room a lot alone, drinking and smoking, she was probably depressed', Enrique said, which 'affected her interest with everyone', he concluded. 'It's funny because she only seemed to come alive at the parties, when she was really drunk', I said, before following up, 'it must have been so difficult to deal with the loss of her husband'. 'Probably this [the drinking and anti-social tendencies] was when from when he died', Enrique said, but 'people don't understand this, Ana and Fernando didn't understand that she was grieving and in a state of depression, they just saw her being idle in their view'. He continued:

Enrique: Anya even asked us, and she wasn't even staying with us, if we could take her children to the park! She took advantage, it's probably why Ana and Fernando asked her to leave, that as well as Christmas was coming and they wanted their family to visit. They said to her in reasonable terms, to at least help around the house or contribute, as she was earning money. But she did neither. She tended to just stay in her room after work, smoke and drink.

Dan: I remember at that party, there was a big argument about that.

Enrique: Yes, because they asked her to leave because she did nothing so she comes to me and asked if she can stay here but we said 'You have to do something, you can't be in your room drinking, you have to keep your mind busy.' Valentyna told her this but no change and even advised me not to take Anya in because she would just be a liability.

Dan: Then she got angry.

Enrique: She just said she was going back to Ukraine, she wanted to stay here on her terms. She was just too selfish, but she wasn't right in the head, too much suffering, very damaged woman in many ways.

It was just as I had documented that night:

> It is nearing midnight, and the partying and drinking has been underway since lunchtime. It is difficult to remember what is being celebrated or even if it is anything other than an opportunity to have a drink and put some music on. Nadia is somehow still playing with Ighor, Milana and Yesenia in the living room and the dog is playfully joining in while Enrique and Belén are outside singing with Valentyna. Anya sits in the corner with a cigarette in her mouth and sways drunkenly from side to side much to the moralistic disappointment of her host family Ana and Fernando who look on and talk about her while they shake their heads. It's only then that Enrique comes over and tries to persuade me to sing with him. 'Is everything OK with Anya', I ask him. 'Look I wasn't

going to tell you but Ana and Fernando have asked her to leave before Christmas and we are trying to persuade her to stay with us in the attic.' 'But there is no room really, is there?' I ask. 'No not really but we offer because we don't want her to go back home because it is fucking dangerous' replies Enrique.

Enrique drifts back off to sing, then just a few minutes later, there is some commotion and Anya storms upstairs crying. Enrique and I follow and knock on the door but all we can hear is a vociferous conversation with someone in Ukrainian. Valentyna goes into the room and we are left outside. 'Best leave it to them', says Enrique, and we go downstairs again. Ten minutes later, a red-eyed Anya appears; this time arguing with Valentyna. The party spirit has certainly halted as the music is paused. Valentyna tells us that Anya wants to return to Kharkiv. 'Who was on the phone?' I ask before Valentyna says, 'her brother who was telling her she is mad to come home to the hell on earth'. We try to console Anya, but she won't let anyone near her and goes back upstairs. I call over Nadia, embrace everyone and decide to call it a night. On the way home, a message comes through on my phone from Oksana who has now been back in Ukraine for a few months. It reads 'after the arrival of the rockets on Tuesday near my house it is difficult, we hold on, our life is on hold in a way'. (Field notes, 'Anya's crisis')

The day Anya left Brunete with her children was truly one of the most emotional days of our lives. Enrique agreed:

'Where are you, Dan? They are leaving in 10 minutes' the message reads from Enrique. For some reason, their departure time has been brought forward. Nadia and I put on our shoes, hurry up the road and towards Enrique's house. The mood is beyond sombre when we arrive and if feels like we are attending their funeral. There is nothing any of us can say and there are only tears between everyone as Anya hugs her best friend Valentyna and embraces all of us before drying her eyes and getting into the taxi. Anya is leaving. Conversation dries up quickly, there are no reliable pleasantries to counter these moments. There are no more distractions to help remedy this situation, there is sadness all around. We give Ighor and Milana presents and they smile reluctantly as they open them. Nadia is particularly emotional and clings onto Milana while Ighor holds me tightly and cries. With that, they get in the car and look on at us crying as the car pulls away. (Field notes, 'Goodbye')

Notes

[1] FRA (2023).
[2] EUI (2023).

[3] International Rescue Committee (2023).
[4] Duray-Parmentier (2023).
[5] Raymen (2023).
[6] Briggs and Dobre (2013).
[7] Briggs (2020).

7

In search of *Slava Ukraïni*

By March 2023 – one year into the conflict – my town's time supporting Ukrainians had concluded. As the French writer Jean-Baptiste Alphonse Karr coined in 1949, *the more things change, the more they stay the same* for the experience of welcoming the Ukrainians seems now a distant memory for the townspeople. The Spanish host families have returned to the daily slog of work, the obligatory summer holiday and their cultural routines. The mayor was re-elected and the council's subsidiary company, Greener Grass, recruited a group of newly arrived Moroccans to tend to the upkeep of public spaces. Some of the people we met went home to endure an unknown resolution to the conflict, while others continue their journey in other European countries hoping for better outcomes.

The future for Europe and the refugee influx

Europe's cultural, political and economic landscape has been profoundly shaped by such conflict and cooperation. The scars of the two world wars, the Cold War's ideological divide, and the subsequent push towards European integration through institutions like the European Union (EU) have all left indelible marks on the continent. The EU emerged as a beacon of peace, economic cooperation and shared values, aiming to prevent the horrors of the 20th century from recurring. And while the postwar period saw Europe commit to a vision of integration and cooperation, fostering economic growth and political stability, the current context is markedly different. The Ukrainian/Russian war on Europe's borders, the rise of nationalism and the surge in migration has tested the resilience of the cosmopolitan project, evidenced in the observations and testimonies of Ukrainian refugees attempting to survive in this small enclave in Spain.

War in Europe, once thought to be a relic of the past, has re-emerged as a pressing concern. The Russian invasion of Ukraine in 2022 shattered the illusion of a peaceful post-Cold War order and brought the spectre of conflict back to the European continent. This war has not only caused widespread devastation and displacement in Ukraine but also underscores the fragility of European stability and the dangers of unresolved historical grievances. It has also exposed the limitations of European security structures, prompting renewed debates about the role of the North Atlantic Treaty Organization, the EU's Common Security and Defence Policy, and the continent's continued and relentless reliance on the United States for military protection/intervention.

Notwithstanding, the conflict in Ukraine has triggered one of the largest refugee crises in Europe since the Second World War, with millions of people such as Oksana and her family fleeing the conflict and seeking refuge in European countries as evidenced in this short sociological diary. This has further placed immense pressure on European governments, humanitarian organisations and local communities – already dealing with the existing challenges posed by migration from other regions, particularly from the Middle East, Africa and South Asia – which have had to attempt to rapidly mobilise resources to support displaced populations. Brunete, a small suburban working-class town on the outskirts of Madrid, found itself in the midst of the refugee influx even if its geographical proximity from Ukraine is significant. The town – like many across Spain – was unprepared for the challenges and, to some degree, was forced to look for solutions to support the new population, even if the systemic barriers meant that many of the women fell into exploitative work opportunities often available through local entrepreneurs.

But the arrival of yet more refugees in Europe also rekindled contentious debates across Europe, fuelling the rise of populist and nationalist movements that often frame migration as a threat to national security, cultural identity and economic stability – even if millions of these people, as well as the Ukrainians in this book, are exploited and end up propping up grey areas of the economy via informal work opportunities. Much like Katya, they contend for survival with a growing number of others in similar situations, adding to the negative competitive feeling of not really getting anywhere and, maybe like Olena and Yana, reason that changing country or area will mark a change in fortune. Very often, though, it doesn't.

The issue of increased migration prompts the issue of integration as a focal point of social and political discourse. On one hand, the successful integration of migrants and refugees can be argued to be crucial for maintaining social cohesion, economic stability and political harmony, however the evidence provided here in this micro-Spanish case study shows what can happen if it is mismanaged, or in the case of the hosting experience, not really managed at all. As hosts, we were operating at best on an ad-hoc basis in the vacuous lack of official and strategic government support and direction. With all good meaning, dealing with these challenges along with geopolitical upheaval, military-industrial complex stimulated conflicts and macro-level change was a little too much for many of us to fathom and, instead, what shone through was the default setting to which we revert to prioritise our own individual needs, and engage our own expectations and ambitions as well as how much our ability to patiently empathise wore thin during times of adversity. Much more so when economic shocks – such as that in the aftermath of the Ukraine/Russia conflict – have the potential to exacerbate existing inequalities as costs rise.

The economic implications of increased migration and the presence of war are profound for Europe. On one hand, migration can contribute to economic growth by filling labour shortages, boosting innovation and addressing demographic challenges such as ageing populations. Notwithstanding, migrants often bring entrepreneurship and valuable skills, such as Valentyna's haberdashery experience and Karina's dentistry know-how. However, more often than not, they also perhaps bring a reluctant willingness to take on jobs that were poorly taken up by the host populations. On the other hand, the economic integration of migrants requires significant investment in education, training and social services. The costs associated with supporting refugees, particularly those fleeing war, can strain public finances, especially in countries already grappling with economic challenges. The unequal distribution of migrants across Europe has also led to tensions between countries, with frontline states like Spain bearing a disproportionate burden. In a country on the frontline of daily arrivals from sub-Saharan Africa, and already tired of dealing with such challenges, Spain at best has a tokenistic interest in investing and providing adequate medium- to long-term support for more refugees[1] – despite its political promises (Chapters 2 and 3). It was always unlikely that the Spanish government would invest much in supporting Ukrainian refugees, especially when the only strategy and willingness to invest in anything refugee-related seems to be around enforcing or improving border security.[2] Solving the refugee conundrum requires international collaboration coupled with a national commitment but there is no money in the coffers for Spanish national debt levels have risen €400 billion in five years and are forecast to continue to increase by a further €300 billion by 2029.[3]

War, displacement and migration have intensified debates about European identity, values and the future of the European project, more so now as the continent grapples with tensions now bubbling in many urban and suburban areas between preserving national identities and embracing multiculturalism. Yet, as this book shows, cultural divergences also highlight the limits of cultural integration, as new diverse populations such as the Ukrainians face the challenges of negotiating their place within European societies. As I have shown, all this became much more pronounced when they arrived traumatised from war and displacement, were suddenly within the confines of a stranger's house, in a country where they weren't familiar with the language or the way of life and in a place where, unbeknown to them, there awaited mountainous levels of bureaucracy to make them legitimate and – irrespective of their emotional state – the subtle expectation that they would be eternally grateful for the help, adapt to the household dynamics, find work and contribute to economically sustain themselves as soon as possible never seemed to disappear.

Makeshift saviours

In the absence of an authentic politics – one which would genuinely seek to adequately facilitate the arrival of tens of thousands of refugees in Spain (Chapter 1), – the Spanish host families' disorientation with their own government's ability to assist in the domestic problems of growing inequality, increased costs and precarious living seemed to form part of the foundation for their scepticism for supporting the Ukrainians. In a context during which the mediascape foisted the latest emotive 'trending social problem', such political cynicism remained consistent throughout the hosting period and, to some degree, seemed to be part of the rationale for helping the Ukrainians: kind of a mindset of *they* [the government] *won't do something / a good job so we will have to do it – we will save the situation.*

Caught up in the media maelstrom, the concept of helping sounded good, and even though many host families made it known in a performative sense on their social media forums how they had taken in Ukrainians,[4] in reality, welcoming refugees from a war-torn country brought to their doorstep the latest of the world's pressing challenges of conflict-related migration and put them on the frontline of intervening in them. It may have also brought some kudos for involving themselves in the cosmopolitan project. *We are one world, one culture* sounds good but the evidence provided in this book shows that their generosity instead brought them too close for comfort to the crude challenges of accommodating people with unknown family tensions, subjective troubles and traumas, from a different culture with a different social outlook on life, with no capacity in the language or knowledge of the country, in a transitional situation which made all of this more volatile.

When the Ukrainians moved in, the Spanish host families displayed sympathy and conceived their guests as 'poor' and 'needy' but this quickly evaporated as they mutely projected their meritocratic expectations on their new guests. Expecting them to show neoliberal endeavour and zeal for the new opportunity was one way of trying to alleviate the advanced feeling of *claustropolitanism*[5] many of the host families started to feel as their daily lives, family relations, everyday routines and spending abilities were ruptured. As some Ukrainian women got work, this attitude gathered momentum but when they saw that, rightly or wrongly, they were putting money aside to rebuild their lives, the indignation only solidified their expectations that they needed to be independent and move on to other housing alternatives. A few hosts even started to feel insecure about the ideological social order being jeopardised as a few of the Ukrainians, such as Yana, settled in too well by developing intimate relationships while the work ethic of a handful saw them earn more than a few of the Spanish host families' collective household income.

The experience instead generated the need to escape the situation they had brought upon themselves and return to the comfort of the same absent political and social status quo. There was no time in the moment to reflect and, even in hindsight as we saw with Bea and Alicia, it was difficult to come to terms with the outcome of their hosting other than that it had been beneficial to them as individuals. To this day, I remain the only person in contact with only a handful of the Ukrainians but everyone else seems to have deposited the experience onto a memory scrapheap. Indeed, the speed with which the Ukrainians came and then went didn't seem to register much in the Spanish host families collective memory.[6]

To open arms and closed opportunities

In this book, I have tried to take the reader close to the Ukrainians' real-life feelings and encounters as they dealt with the sudden separation from their home country, the journey to a place unfamiliar to them and the experiences of navigating a new language, new society and new bureaucratic systems and processes. In the wake of this abrupt transition, and to quell the trauma of the situation, they held on to cultural routines and reproduced as much of their cultural life at home in a new setting. Following *Servant of the People*, for example, was one way of maintaining idealised hope for the future even if, the longer the conflict went on, they stopped following the media and reduced their communications and attention to immediate family and friends. Many of the women I came to know developed significant traumas, some more serious (Anya) than others (Nastia) and it felt there was no time to deal with these emotional undercurrents which many seemed to suppress well into their time in Spain.

Their cultural integration also presented considerable challenges. Despite the relative geographical and cultural proximity of Ukraine to many European countries, integrating into a new country such as Spain involves overcoming language barriers, adapting to different social norms and navigating new educational systems. Programmes aimed at facilitating integration, such as language courses and cultural orientation workshops, though crucial, were insufficiently funded or inconsistently available in Spain. The three-month delay to the commencement of Spanish classes surely didn't aid enthusiasm to learn the language and perhaps impacted commitment to the lessons. In all instances, the state support was woefully inadequate and even our improvised attempts at helping and supporting had also problematic shortcomings. The Spanish host families, even with all good meaning, substantially underestimated the demands of hosting and found it impossible to avoid imprinting their cultural and social expectations on the

Ukrainians. With the backdrop of the increasing cost of living (which, in part, the Spanish attributed to the Russia–Ukraine war) and mismatched cultural expectancies and idiosyncrasies, increased tension was felt between the Ukrainians and Spanish, and this marked the rapid collapse of collective efforts to support them.

This book has also shown that the other primary challenge these young Ukrainian women faced was finding stable employment. Many, like Nastia, Masha, Katya and Karina, arrived in host countries with high levels of education and professional skills yet encountered significant barriers to entering the workforce. Language differences, lack of recognition of Ukrainian qualifications and backward bureaucratic hurdles impede their job prospects. While the book has noted how some countries, such as Poland and Germany, made efforts to streamline the process for recognising foreign qualifications and integrating refugees into the labour market, the case discussed in hand (Spain) shows that these young Ukrainian women were underemployed and had little choice but to take jobs below their skill levels to survive. Evident from Katya and Karina's experiences of 'moving on' from Brunete was that there was supposedly a 'better chance' nearer the city but the only things that awaited them were similar dead-end opportunities, discrimination and further exploitation. When Olena and her family left for Germany in search for a 'better opportunity', all that happened was a sidestep into other informal, precarious economies. Taken together, it is perhaps no wonder that many didn't stay long in Brunete.

Dead ends

As you can see in Figure 7.1, almost all the Ukrainian families we had come to know had either left Spain or, more likely, returned home.

Contact with many of the Ukrainian families who returned to their home country dried up quickly. In the months and years since, and in conversation with various Spanish host families, almost none had much to say on to where their respective family had gone or even if they were dead or alive. Within our circle, this was certainly the case. After their moving and sudden return in December 2022, Anya and her two children, Ighor and Milana, returned to a still volatile and vulnerable Kharkiv. My follow-up messaging received some delayed responses early in 2023 but thereafter appeared long gaps in the communication and many of my messages remained unread for months on end. By the early summer of 2023, I got a response asking me how the book about the conflict was going. 'You could write this book forever, there is no end to what Russia is doing to Ukraine', Anya wrote. She enclosed a photo of Ighor and Milana at a friend's birthday party which was followed up with 'Did you see the video on the internet yesterday? How the Russians shot a Ukrainian prisoner? The last thing he said [the prisoner] was Slava

In search of *Slava Ukraïni*

Figure 7.1: Christmas exodus (December 2022/January 2023)

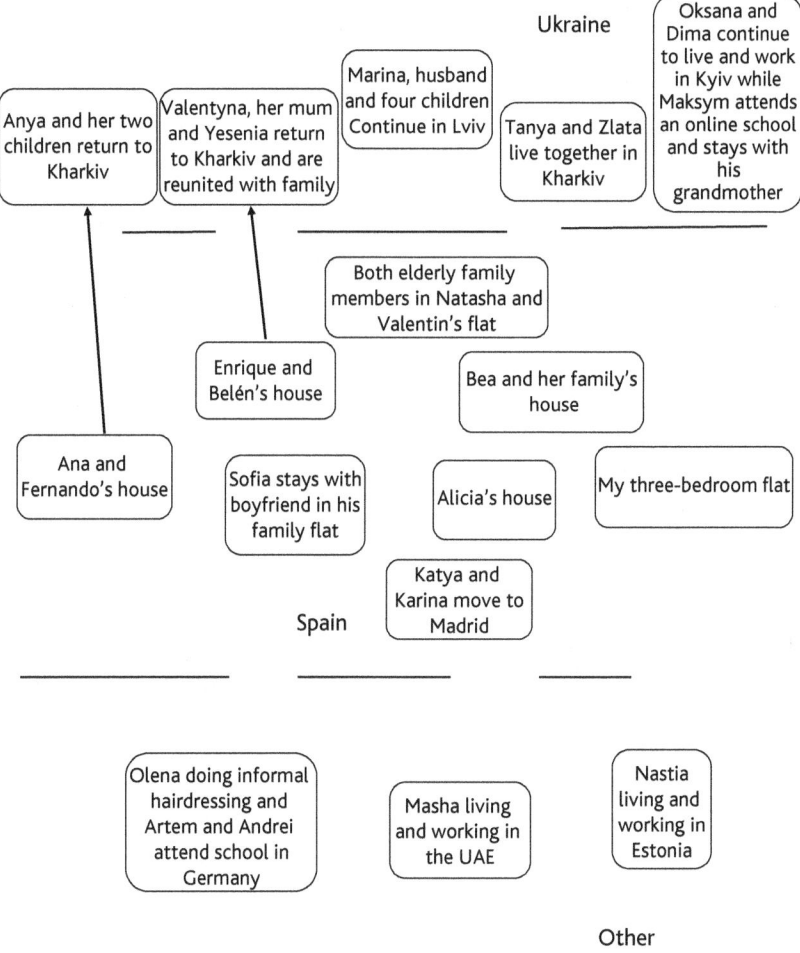

Ukraïni.' Once again, months pass, and the responses dried up until the spring of 2024 when Anya sent me a picture of her parents and her children at an Easter meal. Despite my continued messaging, I've heard nothing since the recent Russian violent revival of interest in Kharkiv which has seen the surrounding city neighbourhoods subject to bombing and missile attacks.

Anya's friend Valentyna continued to rebuild her life along with her husband and a fast-growing Yesenia. When she returned, Valentyna rented an apartment and continued to support her parents. Within a few months, her father died, and her mum's dementia deteriorated. To this day, she continues to care for her mum alongside her own business which now flourishes in the centre of Lviv. The Design and Fabric Studio Valentyna now manages offers customised fashion design from scarves to shirts to elaborate dresses. 'I plan to live here now, it is quiet, it is calm and I am doing well here' her last message to me reads. At least she is thriving in the western part of the country where the danger of attacks is minimal.

By March 2023, Oksana had normalised the daily threat of war. Yet still she made the invitations to me to come to Ukraine. Even in the time I have been writing this book, her intermittent messaging started to become nostalgic about her family's time in Spain. Looking back fondly at their brief time in Brunete, she wrote saying how 'I remember everything too but the last six months I have different feelings here in Kyiv, it is a feeling that this will be like this for a long time.' Over the next few months, her messages only revolved around risks and threats, and on one occasion, when collecting Maksym from the bus station after having spent a week with his grandmother in a faraway town, there was an explosion nearby and they ran for shelter. In another message, she wrote how 'three rockets' were fired over their Kyiv apartment, destroying a whole block of flats in the neighbouring street and sent me a videoclip she recorded of the blazing building.

Failed counteroffensive

There was widespread hope that the planned Ukrainian counteroffensive in 2023, aimed at reclaiming territories occupied by Russian forces, would be the first step towards a slow victory. The operation commenced in the spring of 2023, however it was marked by several key factors contributing to its failure. First, the Ukrainians had hugely underestimated Russia's defensive preparations for Russian forces had fortified their positions extensively, through the use of trenches, minefields and well-coordinated defensive structures. Progress for the advancing Ukrainian troops was hindered because of this, leading to high casualties and slow progress. Furthermore, despite substantial military aid from Western allies, including advanced weaponry and training, Ukrainian forces struggled with supply chain issues and the sheer scale of the territory to be covered. This made the coordination and sustainability of long supply lines problematic as the offensive dragged on.

Notwithstanding, the effectiveness of Ukrainian intelligence and communication was hampered by electronic warfare and cyber-attacks from Russian forces. Disruptions in communication and real-time data sharing hindered the Ukrainian military's ability to adapt quickly to battlefield conditions and coordinate their manoeuvres effectively. Adverse weather conditions and challenging terrain further complicated the offensive for muddy conditions, particularly in the spring, made mobility difficult for Ukrainian armoured units, limiting their ability to advance and making them vulnerable to Russian artillery and drone strikes. Such effective countermeasures not only slowed the Ukrainian advance but also inflicted heavy losses on their units.

Oksana's cause

The protracted nature of the counteroffensive and the high casualty rates affected morale both on the front lines and within Ukrainian society. Now, unlike Vasily Petrovych Goloborodko in *Servant of the People*, there was no fictional story of peace and a corruption-free Ukraine to hold on to, no normal citizen or everyday hero to save them now (Chapter 3). Not even a moving folkloric, award-winning song has been able to save them. When I told Oksana I had finally started writing this book in the summer of 2023, she wrote back a few days later, 'Daniel! Wow 😊 that's good news. You are doing a good job. It is important to tell the whole world about the horrors of war and the lives of Ukrainian refugees who gave up everything for life!' She went on to describe in a bit more detail the latest project on which she had been working. She has been involved in the production of a documentary undertaken by Ukrainian journalists about Putin's kidnapping of Ukrainian children. The documentary, made by *The Kyiv Independent*, charts the disappearance of thousands of children from Mariupol. Since February 2022, the researchers calculated that 19,000 children were 'deported' from Ukraine and move to 'Russian camps' – though a few experts interviewed on the documentary believe this to be more in the region of 100,000. The Russian authorities and media reported their deportation as 'saving them from war'. In the moving documentary, orphan children recall that when trying to flee from Mariupol, they were picked up by various authorities and sent to the Head of Social Services in Donetsk, an area already under Russian control, to be cared for in a network of nine hospitals before being sent into Russia to 'camps'. In fact, thousands of children had previously been brought to these nine hospitals before being deported to Russia because investigative journalists traced the use of this route back to 2014. Rarely parents were reunited with their children, the researchers claimed, and even less so in times of war because they were required to travel into Russian occupied territory in the Donetsk, which was dangerous and risky.[7]

As the new academic year began, Maksym started school again in Kyiv and was reunited with his former basketball club which went on to become Kyiv regional champions, no doubt with the help of Maksym who had overtaken his mum in height. She wrote in early November 2023 how:

> We are all in Kyiv. Maksym has been going to school since the beginning of September [2023], attending a basketball club. Dima and I are working. It has been quiet in Kyiv for the last few weeks. There hasn't been any shelling for three weeks. But the fall season is starting,

so I think the shelling will return. Russia is stockpiling missiles and drones to attack civilian infrastructure on a massive scale. It happened last year. We have to move on, so we are learning to live in war. It is clear that it will last for a long time. (Oksana)

When contact was re-established, the new year had passed and the two-year anniversary of the war was drawing near. I called Oksana one day and she answered from her office, just five minutes' walk from Zelenskyy's government headquarters. She gave me a small, guided tour of the office and the view outside before saying how 'Maksym, he goes to school in this area, I need a special pass to drop and collect him'. Though the air raids had diminished, the university's Arts building had been destroyed close to their apartment in the early spring period. 'It is only 100 metres away', says Oksana, shaking her head. 'My neighbour said it was very bad, they were very scared.' She then says, 'the morning is the most dangerous time as people are out, at work, at school'. Though it seems that Maksym goes to school in the 'most secure area', when the air raid alarms go off, he must head for the basement the same as every other citizen in Kyiv. There isn't a great deal of time spent outside because:

> I am mostly at home or work, yes, its dangerous as this is everyday life, but the sleep is most difficult. If the raids go off, we have to get up and go to the basement. We have only 30 seconds to get to a shelter, it is not enough time, there is not enough warning. I feel tired a lot because of this. (Oksana)

On returning to Ukraine, Oksana travelled a lot for her work to support the journalists visiting Odessa. As recently as January 2024 she described their collective efforts in Odessa as 'very dangerous, more dangerous than Kyiv – the city is all flat now, it is rocks and rubble'. She told me that she continued to work on corruption stories in her unwavering and persistent support of the Ukrainian journalists working in occupied or around battle territory: 'The biggest problem we have with corruption of the war, the bribes, the corruption with arms and weapons. We are working on these projects to expose these things.' Nearly five years into Zelenskyy's premiership and the government continues its ongoing battles with corruption, which Oksana puts down to 'the bad people around Zelenskyy' rather than a dysfunctional political system per se (Chapter 1). Only recently, with the advent of 2024, there was a large scandal regarding spending on weapons. Writing in the *Conversation*, Wolff and Malyarenko noted that '[a] scandal has engulfed the Ukrainian ministry of defence, where 100,000 mortar shells worth about $40m (£31m) were paid for but never delivered. But within days of this story emerging, Ukraine achieved its best-ever ranking in the annual corruption perceptions index compiled by Transparency International (TI)'.[8]

The more things change, the more they stay the same. But beyond the never-ending daily fight Oksana says she must continue to *right* the many *wrongs* in the country, and just seems happy to be with her family. Despite the imminent and daily dangers, she said:

> Dima is happy because I am here with Maksym. It's true we have to be together. I am happy I stay home, but I stay home I feel more safe because I am happy to stay with my country, people who live here and my family. It is important to stay because if everyone leaves, we can't be safe and fight. (Oksana)

Brighter sky, darker city

When the one-year anniversary of the war came around, we all received a message from Masha in our 'Ukrainian Occupiers' WhatsApp group: 'Hi, all. How are you? I'm in the Emirates. It's interesting to be here, big modern country with a lot of possibilities and challenges. Everything is ok but not it's still not home. I am now working on a really interesting new project with Ukrainian bosses on the top.' By the summer of 2023, Masha had moved to Dubai, got her papers, found accommodation and within a short period of time even been promoted. Excitedly, her next communication was that:

> I like being here. I work eight hours a day, the work is not hard and I have already been promoted – then it's up to me to come up with new desserts and manage the staff. All in all, it is a great experience – I take the most of it! (Masha)

As autumn closed in 2023, things still seemed to be going well for Masha and her adaptation to life in Dubai seemed to be almost complete:

> I'm doing great. I'm already used to the weather and 'style of life' in Dubai. I'm missing family but it's ok we can play around and meet somewhere in Europe. The news [about the war] doesn't help us to feel good being far from our families. But we have to be strong and support each other in this horrible time. Peace to all people. And no missiles and bombs over any heads 🙏. (Masha)

When I spoke again with Masha as the second anniversary of the war drew close, things seemed to be different. She connects to me via Zoom from Dubai with a tan and the blue sky in the background. Outside it is about 30 degrees centigrade and the restaurant curtains flap lazily in the wind as a cleaner mops around the tables where she had just finished breakfast. 'This is nothing, it can get up to 50 in the summer, you can't go outside and while Spain was hot but this is something else' she says with a smile. But the smile soon drops even when she starts to describe some of the 'benefits' associated with her tenure in Dubai:

> I like the sea, I can go to the beach, plenty of chill out time, the temperature of the sea. Also everything is convenient, you want something you can get it. If you are young and white, sorry to say this, but you can get promoted quick. There is no issue with age if you work hard. Except the fact that if you are from a certain ethnic background, regardless of age, you are likely to be confined to certain work. (Masha)

She continues:

> Here you get what you want, when you want. You pay. If you want something delivered, you click on the phone and it comes. Like I live in a shared flat which has separated rooms but I can get delivery to my room, I don't have any reason to leave other than to go to work. Same in Estonia, its cold so people go to work and go home. I may not leave my apartment in a few days if I am not working. (Masha)

Yet her upgrade by Dubai standards is slight even if she may be in a better economic position than hundreds of thousands of daily wage workers. We get on to the subject of her quick ascension in her organisation:

Dan: So how is it you have excelled so quickly – apart from your skin colour as you say?

Masha: When I first came and was assistant pastry chef then within a year, I became a pastry chef and then I am now supervising people, four people I now manage. I work in another company which launches new restaurants and work across the different places. It is good but it is a lot of work, responsibilities, long hours. It is good, I am learning and people are learning from me, new ingredients and combinations.

Dan: Does the salary cover your expenditure? I mean for the rent and living costs.

Masha: When I came here, my salary was €1,500. Now I earn €2,000 but the rent is €800 and if you want a studio say, even still shared, maybe a bit more space, this is €1,500! It is not worth

	it because if I do that then I can't afford to leave to see my family as the flights are so expensive.
Dan:	How does that compare with other wages? I mean it sounds like you have a decent job there.
Masha:	Normal chefs earn €1,000 but they are the ones renting bedspaces and sending money home. The people washing the dishes, normally Indians or Pakistanis, earn €500 and rent bedspace, there [are] maybe like 30 in a flat, and send €100 home but this supports their whole family for a month. People are afraid to do anything else because the money means so much to them even if it is exploitative work. These people don't seem to go anywhere because they don't promote people from the 'cheap countries' as they call them.

Even though she had initially been ready to stay in Spain having learnt some of the language and having held out during lengthy asylum processes, when the offer came from another Ukrainian contact to try a new opportunity in the Middle East, she leapt at it. Feeling quite naïve, though, she accepted the offer on the back of a WhatsApp conversation and turned up in Dubai with only €300 and little idea about where to go, how to get work papers and never having met her new boss. 'Within a day, my new boss was able to meet me and the company sorted the working papers out within a week, it wasn't like Spain!' she said. So, the 'big risk', as she describes it, seems to have paid off even if the veneer of working in Dubai is starting to wear thin and the novelty of the glitz and glam image of the city is similarly fading. As I have shown, labour inequality in Spain is extremely prevalent (Chapter 4), but life in the neoliberal hotbed of one of the world's most notoriously rich, disparate and exploitative cities (Chapter 1) is becoming glaringly difficult for her to ignore:

Masha:	There is no nature here, it is all artificial. I mean there is grass but they just buy it and put it in. All the public spaces like this. It's like the people as well. Artificial. They are just kind and nice, 'Hello, how are you' like Americans talk but they are like fake and I hate they treat you like this. It is everything about the place.
Dan:	Why is it like this?
Masha:	Because it's all about service, everyone is a customer. You come to Dubai to work, nothing else. Everyone here is here to work, at all levels. Work, earn money. There are no other relationships.
Dan:	Do you have any friends there?

Masha: It is difficult, in the restaurant there is a few Ukraine people, some from Europe but it is working, it is time we know each other in work. People are either working or at home. There is not much socialising. Do I have friends? I don't know. Some people I know are nice, friendly, they value you but no one comes here for friendship, they come to work and earn money. Everyone is closed. I find myself feeling lonely its why I am on the phone to Nastia each day on FaceTime, on videocall to keep me sane.

Dan: So what is keeping you in Dubai?

Masha: Not much apart from the work. The rate of rents are so high, like for what? In all the buildings there are cockroaches so it's not like you are paying for luxurious buildings, in all buildings, all hotels, fine restaurants. Also people seem to have no money or lots of money. I still don't think I earn a lot of money because I am not able to save much, just pay a lot for rent. I mean I have lunch and dinner in the restaurant so only pay breakfast but even then everything else is so expensive. There are no people in between. You are either very rich or poor.

Family fulcrum

Aside from leaving to have urgent medical treatment and surgery for her back – because healthcare rates were similarly expensive – Masha had only left Dubai three times during her time there. 'She will wait there until the end of the year', Nastia says, 'she will get a better offer from a Europe restaurant, you will see, she will come home' she added, before concluding that the working conditions will eventually influence her to leave: 'all people in Dubai, Arabians, Indians, so many people in one place doing bad paid jobs'. As we saw in Chapter 6, Nastia, considered by her brothers and sisters to be the most settled because she had 'a whole flat' to herself, had moved to Estonia and taken up a job for a tech company dedicated to immersive sporting experiences. She had settled in quickly after arriving in December 2022 and thereafter we received periodic updates in our WhatsApp group. Even though she had managed to get a job like Masha, her early messaging one year into the conflict, echoed her sister's feelings: it was still not 'home': 'I am working in office, it is hard and interesting. Calm. Small city and country. Good but not home. I am use maximum from this period for myself for sure. Later but will see.'

By the summer of 2023, Nastia was established in her sports tech company, having got promoted twice, and getting an additional online job with the Ukrainian under-18 basketball team. The job seemingly going well, she said she was 'in good relations with colleagues' but how they were 'not really friends but good people'.[9] 'At least they pushed me to celebrate my birthday and came to my flat on Sunday to celebrate and bring the flowers', she said, adding 'I feel that they like me, they promote me, they respect me and I changed titles [promotion] but I am not sure if it is friendship exactly'. The promotions have seen steady wage increases which have enabled Nastia to support other members of her family in more precarious positions as well as her parents. For example, Nastia was able to afford to pay for her father's eye surgery so he could continue to work and drive. At this point, Nastia decided to risk her first journey back home to Kyiv, after taking the 33-hour bus from Tallinn to Kyiv via Poland. Because of the geographical spread of the family, she was the only family member able to do this. She recalled that:

Nastia: In my imagination, when I first went back to Kyiv I thought it would be all flattened, destroyed but I was walking around where I used to work in Kyiv centre and I was like wow it is all still here, this monument is still here, people are doing normal things – well it is normal until the air raid signs start.

Dan: Have your parents thought about leaving Ukraine? I mean to visit you for example.

Nastia: Our parents couldn't do nothing, they don't want to change their lives, they couldn't move out, Dad age not allow him and Mum has Russian citizenship so she can't go anywhere, or present herself to anyone. For Mum could be a good option to Poland to meet her brother but didn't want to risk it.

Dan: So you have to periodically risk seeing them, do you worry about this?

Nastia: I worry about them but if I will do this constantly, I will go mad. I remember I stopped doing this in June [2022] in Spain, I was trembling, shaking every night, but then I accepted they want to stay and that it was better to look for opportunities to visit them to go to Kyiv.

As autumn turned to winter in 2023, Nastia wrote to me again about how she was 'able to manage abroad in Estonia' and 'thinking to come home in November – but still no final decision'. When further conflict erupted in between Israel and Gaza in October 2023, Nastia wrote again how 'this makes me more want to see mum and dad, the worlds went crazy!' Like Masha, she took comfort in the FaceTime calls with her siblings and the patchy contact she had with her parents who, in her view, 'bravely continue to work in schools'. When we talked during the spring of 2024, two years into the conflict with Russia, it felt like this was the best possible arrangement for her until there was some resolution in her home country. On connecting with her via videocall, a bright but messy room appears in the background. Some clothes are on a hanger, others are strewn on an unmade bed and various bunches of flowers adorn the room, marking Nastia's 30th birthday:

> Marc will be coming to stay with me as the basketball season closed in Italy and his club has let him go. He will move to another club in autumn and will have completed five years in Italy so he will be entitled to permanent contract when he next signs for a club – it was because he was considered a 'foreigner' that the clubs were just paying him during the season, because outside that he gets no money. No money, and he can't pay rent or food. (Nastia)

The reunion with Marc reminded Nastia of when both he and Masha came for Christmas and New Year 2023: 'it was good as everyone had their own bed but in my apartment we all in the same bed' she says and laughs. 'Simon is too far from us and expensive to get to USA as it is expensive for Masha to leave Dubai', she added, recalling the current family situation. 'When Simon had the opportunity to come to Europe for a tournament I was involved in organisation, I paid for Marc and Masha to come for us to be together … it was only two days, but we have to look for these moments together' she reflects. 'Family is all around the planet', she concluded. The second time Nastia visited Kyiv to see her parents was with Masha so her sister could have the back operation as she was in severe pain. But on the third visit:

Nastia: The third time I go to Kyiv I go to see my parents; I try to go as often as possible. I meet my friend there as well and she tells me that when I come the air raids come [laughs]. Russia prepares massive attacks only when I come or what? I say this because some months nothing happens then there is an onslaught.
Dan: Did you hear the bombs?
Nastia: Yes, I did, I was in basement, I was recording the sounds, the vibrations and sending it to her. I was sleeping in fact and in my head, I thought it was fireworks but then I am realising it is bombs and I ran to basement. It remind me of the first times when we were attacked, my dad was already in the kitchen, for him it is normal now.

Now Nastia had fully settled in Estonia with the confirmation of the renewal of her resident permit to work for another five years. With no pressure to leave, Nastia feels a responsibility to continue to offer and to help find stability for her siblings:

> War makes you think about the things that matter, it matters that I have money to get my father surgery, to pay for Marc to come to Europe to see our parents, this is what matters. You know Marc he also say to me this, he came for Christmas, there was a moment, Christmas Eve [2023], it was the tradition to cook 12 dishes and I was cooking them and he said to me while he was trying the food 'OK Nastia, you are now instead of mum' and it shocked me, then he realised what he say and it was the first time and I didn't feel good about this and I called Masha and she said 'You are like mum, you are our home right now, we come to you, we come home to you'. (Nastia)

Mayoral re-election and precarious work top-up

Meanwhile, back in Brunete, the re-election of the mayor seemed almost inevitable over the summer of 2022 but with the evaporation of cheap labour in the town, the public spaces started to quickly fall into disrepair early in 2023. With no surplus population to pick up the work and a host culture considering it to be far below their standards, pressure mounted on the council. A campaign was devised to attract more Moroccans to Brunete and some cheap housing was made available through the quick refurbishment of some unfinished properties on the outskirts which had originally fallen victim to the 2008 financial crisis. Why didn't the mayor think of this for the Ukrainians? Taking advantage of word of mouth through the town's existing networks, 30 Moroccan families moved to the area to take up these jobs and, by the end of the year, the town's public spaces had returned to their former glory.

Alicia's holiday and Alberto's distant memories of the Ukrainians

> In the early summer heat of 2024, I walk towards the bar on the corner where we used to have the host family meetings. Hoping there is no queue, I go in to order a coffee to take away before I collect my daughter from school. It's empty when I enter but one solemn figure sits at the bar sweating lightly under his straw hat. It is Alberto, Alicia's husband. On ordering the coffee, he greets me and puts his heavy arm around my shoulders to embrace me. 'Wow it's been a while since we have seen each other' he says as he sips his *sol y sombra*, a typical after-meal drink made up of brandy and anise dulce. I ask him how things are with the family. 'Better now the Ukrainians have gone' he tuts and shakes his head.

'My wife is happier as she has her space back and she can go on holiday again.' I say how it seems such a long time ago before my recollections are interrupted with some blunt conclusions of his own: 'The problem is they didn't want to work, they didn't want to graft, they didn't want to try to live here, they couldn't accept our way of life!' he says as he shakes his head continuously and with that I excuse myself to collect Nadia. (Field notes, '*Sol y sombra*')

Even now, the meritocratic mantras of neoliberal expectations resonate in almost every one of Alberto's words. In hindsight, it seems easier to responsibilise the Ukrainians for their 'failed integration' or even their failure to get stable work (Chapters 1 and 4) rather than inspect the brittle commitment of most of the Spanish host families (Chapter 5).

Yana's predicament

Meanwhile, in my flat, as the manuscript for this book verges on its imminent submission:

> Everything I don't fully understand about Yana's circumstances was likely to become clearer today when I took her to the unemployment office. As her money ran dry giving fitness classes and more spurious online work also proved to be unyielding, she made a 'cita' or appointment in the social security offices. She said that she had had to wait more than six weeks for the appointment and will likely have to wait more if they can assist her in any way. We park up in Boadilla Del Monte and walk into the offices, up the stairs, register our arrival with a very disinterested receptionist who doesn't lift her eyes from her mobile phone before waiting in the area opposite to watch her make a long call to her friend. While the receptionist's laughs echo down the corridor, we sit and wait. Five minutes pass. Then ten. Still the receptionist talks and laughs. After 15 minutes, I knock on the social security officers' door and am welcomed in. We didn't need to wait after all.
>
> We sit down and the officer speaks to me in Spanish. She has known Yana for well over a year and spends the first few minutes sighing and shaking her head as she explains how Yana should have learnt Spanish by now and got more formal work. 'There is no use coming to us expecting help if you can't be bothered to learn the language' she says, for example, among other moralising comments, and waves a hand in Yana's direction. It's probably fair to say that Yana has not thrust herself into the language but, at the same time, most of her fitness clients are foreign and tend to speak English. The officer tells me how Yana has not 'taken advantage' of Spanish classes which the council used to put on free at the beginning of

the conflict. 'Much of the support has now been retracted and funding streams and support do not exist for the Ukrainians as they used to' she sort of contentedly laments in a told-you-so fashion. *Just like the support the host families were also offering*, I think to myself. As she is speaking, Yana gradually sits back slightly nervous and seems to just get ready to absorb the moralistic verbal tirade from the worker. I convey everything to her in English and Yana tuts saying 'I have tried to learn' before the officer interrupts her: 'In any case, the best she [Yana] can hope for now if she wants unemployment benefit is to register with them in the central office which is 15 kilometres away, she will need an appointment and there are long waiting times. Even when the appointment comes and she attends, she will need all the right documentation validated, signed and stamped from the respective departments. Then there will be a wait, should be around two months, while this is processed. Then and only then can she apply to us for housing. The housing waiting list and Ukrainians are no longer on the priority list so nothing is guaranteed. If she is lucky, she can get some shared accommodation but the funding is on a month-to-month basis so if someone with a greater need presents we will have to prioritise them. By this we mean, single mothers, victims of domestic violence, for example. Unfortunately, Ukrainians are far down the list now.'

So, in a nutshell, the outlook looks almost impossible. I relay this to Yana whose face remains as much motionless as it does emotionless. She will have to stay with me a bit longer it seems. (Field notes, 'Yana's "benefits"')

Back in the flat, she broke down crying, and in midst of it, revealed how she was determined to make her life in Spain work. She displayed no motivation to return to Ukraine, and, aside from the ongoing war, now cited the continued need for distance from a former partner who had raped her some years ago. Over the next few days, Yana reflected on the situation before deciding that she had exhausted her luck in my area and wanted to move on. She asked if I would help her move to Madrid. 'I can apply for jobs in city, and at least there I think I can get more fitness clients … I can charge less but I think there will be more people', she reasoned, because it was more of a dense urban area, before adding 'but here there is nothing for me and the people in offices won't give me chance for support'. There was a feeling of defeat in her words as she said this and started to look for room rental options in the suburbs. Within a few hours, she found a room to rent in Batán, a rough area of southern Madrid renowned for poor housing and high crime. 'There is a metro stop nearby' she said as she started to pack her bags, once again.

The next day I helped Yana load her bags and food from the fridge into my car before driving her to Batán. Cautious not to get fined for speeding, I drove well below the limit and all the while Yana was quiet during the journey, pensive with a resolute face. We came off the A5, turned into a high-rise block area and follow the GPS location to what would be her fifth new home in Spain since arriving over two years ago. The block we approached looked as tired and as dilapidated as the crumbling pavement below. I parked nearby but it was a hard graft up the stairs to the fourth floor with all her belongings. She knocked on the door and a stern-looking young Polish woman answered in her pyjamas. There wasn't much to see in the flat because all the doors had padlocks and it was only then that we learned that the officially registered two-bedroom flat Yana would share was with three other young women. 'We all work in the city here, generally cleaning but the other girls are not here now' said the Polish woman who scuffed around in her flipflops towards Yana's new room before walking off to finish getting dressed: in the city, everyone is an entrepreneur – even the small-scale flat-owners who take advantage of housing shortages and the saturated insecure precarious work opportunities (Chapters 1 and 4). As we entered Yana's new living quarters, a single bed sat on the left, a cupboard with a door missing stood straight in front of us and a small table and stool sat on the right. 'Right, thank you for help me', she said, as she flung her arms around me before trying to speed up my exit to avoid getting emotional.

As I drove home, it dawned on me that Yana was the last recently arrived Ukrainian to leave Brunete. Our part in these people's lives seemed to now be over, though, as you can see even up until this word, I have tried to follow their lives and decisions ever since. The only Ukrainians who remained in my town were those who had been here for more than 20 years and, as they finished their drinks in the café leaving only the ice to melt, even they ended up wondering what could be taken from the whole experience:

Valentin:	The worst thing was at the [Spanish host] meetings, we just went round in circles, all the time the Spanish complaining then all that stuff in the WhatsApp group.
Natasha:	They [the government/council/authorities] should have done more to join the two communities. There were some good ideas, you [me] had a few, but nothing meaningful came out of it.
Valentin:	That's just it. Nothing much came out of it, coming here [to Brunete], nothing meaningful came out of it. Perhaps your book, but who knows?

Who knows.

Notes
1. Briggs (2020).
2. Briggs (2020).
3. Statista (2024).

4   Thimsen (2022).
5   Redhead (2011).
6   Virilio (2010).
7   *DW News* (2024).
8   Wolff and Marlyenko (2024).
9   Redhead (2011).

References

Abelow, B. (2022) *How the West Brought War to Ukraine: Understanding How U.S. and NATO Policies Led to Crisis, War and the Risk of Nuclear Catastrophe*, Washington, DC: Siland Press.

Adunts, D., Kurlyo, B. and Špeciánová, J. (2022) *Location Choice and Dispersal Policies: Ukrainian War Immigrants in the Czech Republic*, Prague: Research Institute for Labour and Social Affairs.

Albrecht, C. and Panchenko, T. (2022) 'Refugee flow from Ukraine: origins, effects, scales and consequences', *CESifo Forum*, 23(4): 8–16.

Altinay, L., Alrawadieh, Z., Hudec, O., Urbančíková, N. and Evrim Arici, H. (2023) 'Modelling social inclusion, self-esteem, loneliness, psychological distress, and psychological resilience of refugees: does hospitableness matter?', *Journal of Business Research*, 162: Article 113901. https://doi.org/10.1016/j.jbusres.2023.113901

Andrews, J., Isánski, J., Nowak, M., Sereda, V., Vacroux, A. and Vakhitova, H. (2023) 'Feminized forced migration: Ukrainian war refugees', *Women's Studies International Forum*, 99: Article 102756.

Andriewsky, O. (2015) 'Towards a decentred history: the study of the Holodomor and Ukrainian historiography', *East/West: Journal of Ukrainian Studies*, 2(1): 18–52.

Babakova, O., Fiałkowska, K., Kindler, M. and Zessin-Jurek, L. (2022) 'Who is a "true" refugee? On the limits of Polish hospitality', *CMR Spotlight*, 6(41): 1–15.

BBC (2022) 'Ukraine war: why is control of Kherson so important?', *BBC*, 8 November 2022. Available at: https://www.bbc.com/news/world-63511626 (accessed 24 August 2024).

Benjamin, M. and Davies, N. (2022) *War in Ukraine: Making Sense of a Senseless War*, New York: OR Books.

Briggs, D. (2020) *Climate Changed: Refugee Border Stories and the Business of Misery*, London: Routledge.

Briggs, D. (2022) 'Breaking the shackles of academic capitalism: academic life, liberation and ethnographic innovation', in R. Faria and M. Dodge (eds) *Qualitative Research in Criminology: Cutting Edge Methods*, Springer, pp 19–37.

Briggs, D. and Dobre, D. (2013) *Culture and Immigration in Context: An Ethnography of Romanian Migrant Workers in London*, London: Palgrave Macmillan.

Briggs, D. and Monge Gamero, R. (2017) *Dead End Lives: Drugs and Violence in the City Shadows*, Bristol: Policy Press.

Briggs, D., Ellis, A., Lloyd, A. and Telford, L. (2021) *Researching the COVID-19 Pandemic: A Critical Blueprint for the Social Sciences*, Bristol: Bristol University Press.

References

Briggs, D., Telford, L., Ellis, A. and Lloyd, A. (2023) *The New Futures of Exclusion: Life in the COVID-19 Aftermath*, London: Palgrave Macmillan.

Brücker, H., Ette, A., Grabka, M., Kosyakova, Y., Niehues, W., Rother, N., et al (2023) *Ukrainian Refugees in Germany: Evidence From a Large Representative Survey*, Berlin: Federal Institute for Population Research.

Buchcik, J., Kovach, V. and Adedeji, A. (2023) 'Mental health outcomes and quality of life of Ukrainian refugees in Germany', *Health and Quality of Life Outcomes*, 21: Article 23.

Carlsen, C., Gårdhus, T. and Toubøl, J. (2023) 'Ukrainian refugee solidarity mobilization online', *European Societies*. DOI: 10.1080/14616696.2023.2177704

Carlsen, H.B. and Toubøl, J. (2023) 'The refugee solidarity movement between humanitarian support and political protest', in D.A. Snow, D. Della Porta and D. McAdam (eds) *The Wiley-Blackwell Encyclopedia of Social and Political Movements*, Hoboken: Wiley-Blackwell.

Catani, C., Wittmann, J., Schmidt, T.L., Wilker, S., Neldner, S. and Neuner, F. (2023) 'School-based mental health screenings with Ukrainian adolescent refugees in Germany: results from a pilot study', *Frontiers in Psychology*, 14: Article 1146282. doi: 10.3389/fpsyg.2023.1146282

Council of Europe (2018) *Action against Economic Crime Cooperation Highlights 2018*, Geneva: Council of Europe.

De la Fuente, V. and Pinilla, K. (2023) 'Distrust, fear and hate: the drivers of Spain's 23J campaign', *Institute for Strategic Dialogue*, 21 July. Available at: https://www.isdglobal.org/digital_dispatches/distrust-fear-and-hate-the-drivers-of-spains-23j-campaign/ (accessed 25 August 2024).

Dunn, C. and Kaliszewska, E. (2023) 'Distributed humanitarianism', *American Ethnologist*, 50: 19–29.

Duray-Parmentier, C. (2023) 'Stress factor related to the reception of Ukrainian refugees and hosts in Europe', *International Journal of Complementary & Alternative Medicine*, 15(5): 274–5.

DW News (2024) 'Ukrainian children – stolen by Russia', *YouTube*. Available at: https://www.youtube.com/watch?v=-4c-baj28x0 (accessed 20 February 2024).

Eichensehr, K. (2022) 'Contemporary practice of the United States', *AJIL*, 116: 595–9.

Enríquez, C. (2022) *The Welcome Given to Ukrainian Refugees: Some Challenges and Uncertainties*, ARI 31/2022 (English version), 18 April, Madrid: Elcano Royal Institute.

Escrivá, J. (2022) 'Around 25,000 Ukrainian refugees have arrived in Spain so far, claims minister', *Spain in English*, 21 March. Available at: https://www.spainenglish.com/2022/03/21/around-25000-ukrainian-refugees-have-arrived-in-spain-so-far-claims-minister/ (accessed 15 July 2024).

EUI (2023) *Analysis on the Temporary Protection Directive and Its Implications for the Future EU Asylum Policy*, Rome: European Union.

European Commission (2024) 'Commission proposes new measures on skills and talent to help address critical labour shortages', *European Commission Press Release*, 15 November. Available at: https://ec.europa.eu/commission/presscorner/detail/en/ip_23_5740 (accessed 15 November 2024).

Eurostat (2023) 'Over 4.3 million people under temporary protection', *Eurostat Press Release*, 8 February. Available at: https://ec.europa.eu/eurostat/web/products-eurostat-news/w/ddn-20240208-1#:~:text=On%2031%20December%202023%2C%20Ukrainian,20.6%25)%20of%20the%20total (accessed 15 July 2024).

Fegert, J.M., Diehl, C., Leyendecker, B., Hahlweg, K. and Prayon-Blum, V. (2018) 'Scientific Advisory Council of the Federal Ministry of Family Affairs, Senior, Citizens, Women and Youth. Psychosocial problems in traumatized refugee families: overview of risks and some recommendations for support services', *Child Adolescent Psychiatry Mental Health*, 12: 1–8.

Friedman, T. (1999) 'Manifesto for the fast world', *New York Times*, 18 March. Available at: https://www.nytimes.com/1999/03/28/magazine/a-manifesto-for-the-fast-world.html (accessed 15 July 2024).

FRA (2023) *Fleeing Ukraine: Displaced Peoples Experiences in the EU*, Luxembourg: European Union.

Global Attitudes Survey (2018) *Spring 2018 Global Attitudes Survey*, Washington, DC: Pew Research Center.

Gomza, I. (2022) 'The war in Ukraine: Putin's inevitable invasion', *Journal of Democracy*, 33(3): 23–30.

Gotz, E. and Staun, J. (2022) 'Why Russia attacked Ukraine: strategic culture and radicalized narratives', *Contemporary Security Policy*, 43(3): 482–97.

Gradus (2022) *Public Reports: Gradus Research Company*. Available at: https://gradus.app/en/open-reports/ (accessed 15 July 2024).

Graziosi, A. (2004) 'The Soviet 1931–1933 famines and the Ukrainian Holodomor: is a new interpretation possible, and what would its consequences be?', *Harvard Ukrainian Studies*, 27(1/4): 97–115.

Gromadzki, J. and Lewandowski, P. (2022) 'Refugees from Ukraine on the Polish labour market', *Ubezpieczenia Społeczne. Teoria i praktyka* nr 4/2022. Polish Economic Institute in Warsaw.

Hall, S. (2012) *Theorizing Crime and Deviance: A New Perspective*, London: SAGE.

Harmash, O. (2023) 'Recalling Bucha deaths, Zelenskiy describes "horrific" year in Kyiv region', *Reuters*, 30 March. Available at: https://www.reuters.com/world/europe/recalling-bucha-deaths-zelenskiy-describes-horrific-year-kyiv-region-2023-03-30/ (accessed 9 April 2024).

Human Rights Watch (2023) 'Ukraine: Russian forces' trail of death in Bucha', *Human Rights Watch*. Available at: https://www.hrw.org/news/2022/04/21/ukraine-russian-forces-trail-death-bucha (accessed 9 April 2024).

ILO (2021) *ILO Global Estimates on International Migrant Workers: Methodology and Results*, Geneva: ILO.

INE (2022) *Economic Activity, Employment and Unemployment in Spain*, Madrid: INE.

International Rescue Committee (2023) *IRC Poland Protection Monitoring Report September to December 2023*, Brussels: IRC.

Jankowski, M. and Gujski, M. (2022) 'Editorial: the public health implications for the refugee population, particularly in Poland, due to the war in Ukraine', *Medical Science Monitor*, 28: e936808.

Johnson, R. (2022) 'Dysfunctional warfare: the Russian invasion of Ukraine 2022', *The US Army War College Quarterly: Parameters*, 52(2): 5–19.

Jones, L. (2022) 'Ukraine: the reality of sovereignty', *The Northern Star*, 25 March. Available at: https://thenorthernstar.online/2022/03/25/ukraine-and-the-reality-of-sovereignty/ (accessed 15 July 2024).

Kas'ianov, G. (2010) 'The Holodomor and the building of a nation', *Russian Politics and Law*, 48(5): 25–47.

Klein, N. (2007) *The Shock Doctrine: The Rise of Disaster Capitalism*, New York: Penguin.

Koroutchev, R. (2023) 'Ukrainian migration during the first year after the beginning of the Russian armed conflict in 2022', *Journal of Liberty & International Affairs*, 9: 164.

La Moncloa (2022) 'Pedro Sánchez underlines Spain's commitment and solidarity with the 110,000 refugees arriving from Ukraine: "We are going to give them all the protection and opportunities we can"', 8 April. Available at: https://www.lamoncloa.gob.es/lang/en/presidente/news/Paginas/2022/20220408_visit-to-barcelona.aspx (accessed 23 August 2024).

La Moncloa (2023) 'Spain exceeds 170,000 temporary protections for Ukrainian refugees one year after the activation of the mechanism', 3 October. Available at: https://www.lamoncloa.gob.es/lang/en/gobierno/news/Paginas/2023/20230310_ukrainian-refugees.aspx (accessed 15 July 2024).

Lee, A., Khaw, F., Lindman, A. and Juszczyk, G. (2023) 'Ukraine refugee crisis: evolving needs and challenges', *Public Health*, 217: 41–5.

Lintner, T., Diviák, T., Šeďová, K. Hlado, P. (2023) 'Ukrainian refugees struggling to integrate into Czech school social networks', *Humanities Social Science Communications*, 10: 1–11.

Lloyd, A. (2018) *The Harms of Work: An Ultra-Realist Account of the Service Economy*, Bristol: Bristol University Press.

Mass, W. (2013) 'Holodomor: Stalin's holocaust in the Ukraine: this is the 80th anniversary of the Holodomor, Josef Stalin's intentional plan to starve to death much of the Ukrainian population. The death toll likely equaled that of the Nazis', *The New American*, 29(21): 36–8.

Matuszak, S. (2012) 'The oligarchic democracy: the influence of business groups on Ukrainian politics', *OSW Studies*, 42: 1–112.

Mazhak, I., Paludo, A. and Sudyn, D. (2023) 'Self-reported health and coping strategies of Ukrainian female refugees in the Czech Republic', *European Societies*, 26(2): 411–37.

Mbah, R. and Wasum, D. (2022) 'Russian-Ukraine 2022 war: a review of the economic impact of Russian-Ukraine crisis on the USA, UK, Canada, and Europe', *Advances in Social Sciences Research Journal*, 9(3): 144–53.

Mearsheimer, J. (2014) 'Why the Ukraine crisis is the west's fault', *Foreign Affairs*, 93(5): 77–89.

Mearsheimer, J. (2022) 'The causes and consequences of the Ukraine crisis', *The National Interest Magazine*, 23 June. Available at: https://nationalinterest.org/feature/causes-and-consequences-ukraine-crisis-203182 (accessed 15 July 2024).

Mitchell, B. and Fazi, T. (2017) *Reclaiming the State: A Progressive Vision of Sovereignty for a Post-Neoliberal World*, London: Pluto Press.

Molikevych, R. (2023) 'Ukrainian forced migrants in the Czech Republic: situation and living conditions', conference paper presented at 9th SWS International Scientific Conference on Social Sciences, ISCSS 2022.

Mulska, O., Levytska, O., Panchenko, V., Kohut, M. and Taras, V. (2020) 'Causality of external population migration intensity and regional socio-economic development of Ukraine', *Problems and Perspectives in Management*, 18(3): 426–37.

Murphy, A., Fuhr, D., Roberts, B., Jarvis, C., Tarasenko, A. and McKnee, M. (2022) 'The health needs of refugees from Ukraine', *British Medical Journal*, 377: o864: http://dx.doi.org/10.1136/bmj.o864

National Statistics Institute (2022) *Standard of Living Conditions Report, August 2022*, Madrid: National Statistics Institute.

Nehring, H. (2022) 'A short history of Ukraine's relationship with the European Union', *The Conversation*, 2 May. Available at: https://theconversation.com/a-short-history-of-ukraines-relationship-with-the-european-union-178350 (accessed 11 July 2024).

OECD (2023) *What We Know about the Skills and Early Labour Market Outcomes of Refugees from Ukraine*, Paris: OECD.

O'Mahony, J. (2023) 'Spanish bureaucracy leaves Ukrainians waiting for cash help', *AP News*, 3 March. Available at: https://apnews.com/article/ukraine-war-refugees-spain-b03b0473c4adc3a7fb641d0a92a5e6fa (accessed 15 July 2024).

Onuch, O. and Hale, H.E. (2017) 'Capturing ethnicity: the case of Ukraine', *Post-Soviet Affairs*, 34(2–3): 84–106.

Oppedal, B. and Idsoe, T. (2015) 'The role of social support in the acculturation and mental health of unaccompanied minor asylum seekers', *Scandinavian Journal of Psychology*, 56: 203–11.

Ozili, P. (2022) 'Global economic consequence of Russia invasion of Ukraine'. http://dx.doi.org/10.2139/ssrn.4064770

Panchenko, T. (2022) 'Prospects for integration of Ukrainian refugees into the German labor market: results of the ifo online survey', *CESifo Forum*, 23(4): 67–75.

Panchenko, T. and Poutvaara, P. (2022) *Intentions to Stay and Employment Prospects of Refugees from Ukraine*, Economic Policy Brief, No. 46, Munich: CESifo GmbH.

Parenti, C. (2011) *Tropic of Chaos: Climate Change and the New Geography of Violence*, New York: Basic Books.

Pertek, S., Kuznetsova, I. and Kot, M. (2022) *'Not a single safe place': The Ukrainian Refugees at Risk: Violence, Trafficking and Exploitation. Findings from Poland and Ukraine*, Research Report, Birmingham: University of Birmingham.

Politi, E., Gale, J., Roblain, A., Bobowik, M. and Green, E. (2023) 'Who is willing to help Ukrainian refugees and why? The role of individual prosocial dispositions and superordinate European identity', *Journal of Community Applied Social Psychology*, 33: 940–53.

Pop-Eleches, G. and Robertson, G.B. (2018) 'Identity and political preferences in Ukraine – before and after the Euromaidan', *Post-Soviet Affairs*, 34(2–3): 107–18.

Putin, V. (2021) 'On the historical unity of Russians and Ukrainians', Press Release, 12 July. Available at: http://en.kremlin.ru/events/president/news/66181 (accessed 15 July 2024).

Putin, V. (2022) Address by the President of the Russian Federation, 21 February. Available at: http://en.kremlin.ru/events/president/news/67828 (accessed 15 July 2024).

Rashid, A. (2023) 'As the war in Ukraine drags on, America's arms industry reaps the profits', *Analyst News*, 17 May. Available at: https://www.analystnews.org/posts/as-the-war-in-ukraine-drags-on-americas-arms-industry-reaps-the-profits (accessed 15 July 2024).

Raymen, T. (2023) *The Enigma of Social Harm: The Problem of Liberalism*, London: Routledge.

Redhead, S. (2011) *We Have Never Been Postmodern: Theory at the Speed of Light*, Edinburgh: Edinburgh University Press.

Rizzi, D., Ciuffo, G., Sandoli, G., Mangiagalli, M., de Angelis, P., Scavuzzo, G., et al (2022) 'Running away from the war in Ukraine: the impact on mental health of internally displaced persons (IDPs) and refugees in transit in Poland', *International Journal of Environmental Research and Public Health*, 19: Article 16439. https://doi.org/10.3390/ijerph192416439

Rodriguez, L. (2022) 'Why do refugee women from Ukraine face unique risks of violence and exploitation?', *Global Citizen*, 6 April. Available at: https://www.globalcitizen.org/en/content/ukrainian-ref¬ugee-women-exploitation-violence (accessed 15 July 2024).

Sakwa, R. (2014) *Frontline Ukraine: Crisis in the Borderlands*, New York: Tauris.

Sakwa, R. (2021) *Deception: RussiaGate and the New Cold War*, Lanham: Lexington Books.

Schrooten, M., Claeys, J., Debryne, P., Deleu, H., Geldof, D., Gulinck, N., et al (2023) *#FreeSpot. Private Accommodation of Ukrainian Refugees in Belgium*, Brussels: Social Work Research Centre & Centre for Family Studies (Odisee University of Applied Sciences).

Siriwardhana, C., Ali, S., Roberts, B. and Stewart, R. (2014) 'A systematic review of resilience and mental health outcomes of conflict-driven adult forced migrants', *Conflict and Health*, 8: 1–14.

Spiegel, P. (2022) 'Are the health systems of EU countries hosting Ukrainian refugees ready to adapt?', *The Lancet*, 16 September. https://doi.org/10.1016/S2666-7568(22)00197-0

Stark, R. (2010) 'Holodomor, famine in Ukraine 1932–1933: a crime against humanity or genocide?', *Irish Journal of Applied Social Studies*, 10(1): Article 2. doi:10.21427/D7PQ8P

Statista (2024) 'Spain: national debt from 2019 to 2029', *Statista*, 16 August. Available at: https://www.statista.com/statistics/270411/national-debt-of-spain/ (accessed 5 May 2024).

Taras, K. (2008) 'Oligarchs wield power in Ukrainian politics', *Eurasia Daily Monitor*, 5(125).

TeleMadrid (2013) 'Brunete entrega a domicilio las heces de los perros que sus dueños no recogen de la calle', *TeleMadrid*, 4 June. Available at: https://www.telemadrid.es/noticias/madrid/Brunete-entrega-domicilio-perros-recogen-0-1470752929--20130604023619.html (accessed 24 July 2024).

TeleMadrid (2017) 'El juez de la Púnica imputa al alcalde de Brunete por los contratos con Cofely', *TeleMadrid*, 5 October. Available at: https://www.telemadrid.es/noticias/madrid/Punica-alcalde-Brunete-contratos-Cofely-0-1945905392--20171005072314.html (accessed 24 July 2024).

TeleMadrid (2019) 'Brunete impartirá formación profesional para bomberos y efectivos de Protección Civil', *TeleMadrid*, 7 March. Available at: https://www.telemadrid.es/noticias/madrid/Brunete-impartira-profesional-Proteccion-Civil-0-2101289855--20190307101323.html (accessed 24 July 2024).

TeleMadrid (2020) 'El jurado declara culpables de cohecho al exalcalde de Brunete y a una policía local', *TeleMadrid*, 16 December. Available at: https://www.telemadrid.es/programas/telenoticias-2/declara-culpables-cohecho-exalcalde-Brunete-2-2296290396--20201216091315.html (accessed 24 July 2024).

TeleMadrid (2023) 'Brunete se queda sin piscina de verano', *TeleMadrid*, 1 August. Available at: https://www.telemadrid.es/noticias/madrid/Brunete-se-queda-sin-piscina-de-verano-0-2583641630--20230801121955.html (accessed 24 July 2024).

Telford, L. (2022) *English Nationalism and its Ghost Towns*, Abingdon: Routledge.

Terol, A. (2022) 'Ukrainian refugees found shelter in Spain's empty hotels. But then, tourists came back', *The World*, 6 July. Available at: https://theworld.org/stories/2022/07/06/ukrainian-refugees-found-shelter-spain-s-empty-hotels-then-tourists-came-back (accessed 15 July 2024).

Thimsen, A.F. (2022) 'What is performative activism?', *Philosophy and Rhetoric*, 55(1): 83–9.

Trebesch, C., Antezza, A., Bushnell, K., Dyussimbinov, Y., Frank, A., Frank, P., et al (2023) 'The Ukraine support tracker: which countries help Ukraine and how?', *Kiel Working Paper, No. 2218*, Kiel Institute for the World Economy (IfW Kiel), Kiel.

Turrini, G., Purgato, M., Ballette, F., Nose, M., Ostuzzi, G. and Barbui, C. (2017) 'Common mental disorders in asylum seekers and refugees: umbrella review of prevalence and intervention studies', *International Journal of Mental Health Systems*, 11: 1–14.

UNHCR (2022) 'UNHCR welcomes Spain's swift and broad implementation of Temporary Protection Directive for refugees from Ukraine in Spain', *UNHCR Briefing*, 17 March. Available at: https://www.acnur.org/noticias/unhcr-welcomes-spains-swift-and-broad-implementation-temporary-protection-directive (accessed 15 July 2024).

Van Halm, I. and Du, M. (2022) 'Investigations into Ukrainian mass graves highlight the devastating cost of Russia's war', *The New Statesman*, 30 November. Available at: https://www.newstatesman.com/world/europe/ukraine/2022/11/ukraine-mass-graves-russia-war-cost (accessed 29 August 2024).

Varshalomidze, T. (2019) 'Volodymyr Zelenskyy wins Ukraine's presidential vote', *AlJazeera*, 22 April. Available at: https://www.aljazeera.com/news/2019/4/22/volodymyr-zelenskyy-wins-ukraines-presidential-vote (accessed 15 July 2024).

Virilio, P. (2010) *The Great Accelerator*, London: Polity Press.

Winlow, S. and Hall, S. (2022) *The Death of the Left: Why We Must Begin from the Beginning Again*, Bristol: Policy Press.

Winlow, S., Hall, S., Treadwell, J. and Briggs, D. (2015) *Riots and Political Protest: Notes from the Post-Political Present*, London: Routledge.

Winlow, S., Hall, S. and Treadwell, J. (2017) *The Rise of the Right: English Nationalism and the Transformation of Working-Class Politics*, Bristol: Policy Press.

Wolff, S. and Marlyenko, T. (2024) 'Ukraine war: corruption scandals and high-level rifts could become an existential threat as Kyiv asks for more military aid', *The Conversation*, 1 February. Available at: https://theconversation.com/ukraine-war-corruption-scandals-and-high-level-rifts-could-become-an-existential-threat-as-kyiv-asks-for-more-military-aid-222432#:~:text=A%20scandal%20has%20engulfed%20the,by%20Transparency%20International%20(TI) (accessed 14 May 2024).

Yıldız, T. (2023) 'The European Union–Russia–Ukraine triangle: historical background of relations, Russia–Ukraine war, and future prospects', in A. Günar and D. Saygın (eds) *The European Union in the Twenty-First Century*, Leeds: Emerald Publishing Limited, pp 195–210.

Yurchenko, Y. (2017) *Ukraine and the Empire of Capital: From Marketisation to Armed Conflict*, London: Pluto Press.

Žižek, S. (2009) *First as Tragedy, then as Farce*, London: Verso Books.

Index

Page numbers in *italic* type refer to figures.

A

activism, 'performative' 93
Adrian (research participant) 51, 83–4, 85, 109
Afghanistan 11, 36
Africa, migration to Europe from 116
Al Qaeda 13
Alberto (research participant) 35, *35*, *51*, 72, 77, *77*, 95, 98, 104, 131–2
Alicia (research participant) 29–30, 30–1, 34, 35, 51, 64, 72, 73, 74, 75, 76, 77, 79, 80, 81–2, 83, 88, 91, 96–100, 104, *105*, 119, *121*, 131–2
Ana (research participant) 76, 77, 83, 85, 86, 88, 91–2, 111, 112, 113, *121*
Andrei (research participant) 23, 35, *35*, 51, *51*, 72, *121*
Anya (research participant) 51, 67, 68–9, 75, 76, 77, 78, 83, 85, 86, 90, *105*, 110, 111, 120–1, *121*
  crisis 111–13
arms sales 11–12
  corruption scandal in Ukraine 124–5
  Western military support for Ukraine 25
Artem (research participant) 23, 35, *51*, 72, *121*
'Association Trio' (Georgia, Moldova, Ukraine) 10

B

barbarism, and the West-Russia relationship 13
Battle for Brunete, 1937 31
Bea (research participant) 29–30, 30–1, 34, 35, 51, 70, 71, 72, 73, 74, 75, 76, 81, 82, 86, 87, 91, 96–100, *105*, 119, *121*
Belén (research participant) 36, 51, 62, 70, 76, 77, 78, 79, 80–5, 88, *105*, 109–10, 112, *121*
Belgium, Ukrainian refugees in 28
Biden, Joe 43
borshch 44–5
BRICS (Brazil, Russia, India, China, South Africa) 13
Brunete 1–2, *2*
  corruption 33
  political, economic and social context 31–4
  Ukrainian refugees in 2–5, *3*, 29–31, 116
    author's experience of hosting 16–17, 40–50

Brunete Ukrainian Refugee Association 73–4
bureaucracy and administrative processes 53–6
childcare issues 68–70, 75, 90, 97–8, 110–11
cultural integration 4, 53, 70, 78–86, 93, 98, 116, 119–20
education 53, 54, 57–8, 119
employment 4, 53, 59–66, 67–8, 101–3, 116, 118–19, 125–8
experiences of invasion 22–3, 42–3
hosting and support of 34–7, 64, 65–7, 70, 73–4, 75–94, 95, 96–101, 106, 116–17, 119–20
protest marches 71
return to Ukraine 4–5, 88, 95, 108–9, 111, 115, 120–2, 134
Spanish language learning 53, 70–1, 120, 132–3
Bucha, war crimes 43
Bulgaria, NATO membership 8
Bush, George W. 9

C

Canada, Ukrainian refugees in 26
'Cassette Scandal' 7
children
  childcare issues, Ukrainian refugees in Brunete 68–70, 75, 90, 97–8, 110–11
  Russian kidnapping of Ukrainian children 123
Christina (research participant) 51
claustropolitanism 14–15, 118
Cold War 12, 13
Common Security and Defence Policy, EU (European Union) 115
corruption
  Brunete, Spain 33
  Ukraine 6–7, 8, 12, 24, 124–5
cosmopolitanism 14–15
Council of Europe 12
covert ethnographies 18
COVID-19 pandemic 13, 26, 27, 87
Crimea 6, 66
  Russian annexation, 2014 9–10, 16, 23, 24
cultural integration
  limits of 117
  Ukrainian refugees in Brunete 4, 53, 70, 78–86, 93, 98, 116, 119–20

145

cyber warfare 11
Czech Republic, Ukrainian refugees in 26, 27, 46

D

defence spending, and neoliberalism 11–12
Dima (research participant) 37, 46–7, 57, *105*, 108, *121*, 123, 125
Donbas 7, 24, 49
Donetsk 24, 123
dromology 15
drones, military use of 11
Dubai, Masha's employment in 125–8
Duray-Permentier, C. 28–9, 53, 86–7

E

Eastern Partnership, EU (European Union) 10
Economic and Humanitarian Academy, Warsaw 96
education, Ukrainian refugees in Brunete 53, 54, 57–8, 119
employment 14, 61–2
  population decline, and the labour market 61
  Ukrainian refugees in Brunete 4, 53, 59–66, 67–8, 101–3, 116, 118–19, 125–8
Enrique (research participant) 36, 51, 62, 76, 77, 80–5, 86, *105*, 109–10, 111–12, 112–13, *121*
Escrivá, José Luis 30
Estonia
  Nastia's employment in 107–8, *121*, 126, 128–31, 130–1
  NATO membership 8
ethics, and social science research 18
EU (European Union) 115
  Common Security and Defence Policy 115
  Eastern Partnership 10
  European Union-Ukraine Association Agreement 23
  relationship with Ukraine 8, 10, 23–4, 25
  Russia's annexation of Crimea, 2014 23
  Temporary Protection Directive 26
  Ukrainian migrants to 16
  Ukrainian refugees in 26, 28
'Euromaidan' protests 7–8, 23
Europe
  impact and implications of Russian war on Ukraine 115–18
  military and security dependence on the US 116
European Union-Ukraine Association Agreement 23
exploitation/sexual violence risk to Ukrainian refugees 29

F

famine 5–6
Fazi, T. 12, 61

Fernando (research participant) 76, 77, 82, 85, 111, 112, 113, *121*
Franco, General 31
Friedman, Thomas 12

G

Gaza/Israel conflict, 2023 129
gender roles, cultural differences in 53
General Dynamics 25
Georgia
  'Association Trio' 10
  Russian invasion of 9
Germany, Ukrainian refugees in 26, 27, 104, 120
globalisation 11
Gloria (research participant) 82, 88–9
Goloborodko, Vasily Petrovych *(Servant of the People)* 48–50, 123
Gongadze, Georgiy 7, 8
Gradus Research 45
Graziosi, Andrea 5–6
Greener Grass 67–8, 71, 115

H

Hall, S. 15, 84
Hannan, Daniel 25
Holdomor ('death by hunger') 5–6
hosting and support of Ukrainians in Brunete 34–7, 66–7, 116–17, 118–19
  cost of living issues 82, 86–8, 89, 92, 117, 120
  resentments and tensions in host family relationships 64, 65–6, 70, 73–4, 75–94, 95–100, 106, 109–13, 119–20
Human Rights Watch 43

I

Ighor (research participant) 68, 69, 76, 83, 84, 86, 111, 113, 120
inequality 13, 14
informed consent, in research 18–19
International Labour Organization 61
International Rescue Committee, Protection Monitoring Report, Poland 96
Iraq 36
Islamic State 13
Israel/Gaza conflict, 2023 129

J

Jardinería (gardening) 67–8, 71, 76, 78, 103
Jones, L. 6

K

Karina (research participant) 2, 20, 22, 51, *51*, 77, 97, 101–4, *105*, 120, *121*
Karr, Jean-Baptiste Alphonse 115
Katya (research participant) 20, 22–3, 35, 51, 72, 97, 101–4, *105*, 116, 120, *121*
Kharkiv 1, 45, 50–1, 66, 103–4, 120, 121

Index

Kherson 65, 66
Khrushchev, Nikita 6
Kravchuk, Leonid 7
Kuchma, Leonid 7, 8
Kyiv Independent, The 123
Kyiv 43, 45, 122, 123–4, 129, 130

L

La Caixa Foundation 30
language
  online translation tools 44, 45
  Ukrainians' learning of Spanish language 53, 70–1, 120, 132–3
  Ukrainians' rejection of Russian language 46
Latin America, migrants to Spain 32
Latvia, NATO membership 8
Lithuania, NATO membership 8
Lockheed Martin 25
Luhansk 24

M

Maksym (research participant) 37, 40–1, 42–3, 45, 46, 55–8, 62, 72, 77, 80, 84, 86, 100, *105*, 108, *121*, 122, 123–4, 125
Malyarenko, T. 124
Maria (research participant) 70–1
Marina (research participant) 36, *51*, 76, 77, 81, *105*, 109, 110–11, *121*
Mariupol 65, 123
Masha (research participant) 37, 40, 41–3, 44, 45, 47, 58, 59–60, 71, 72, 105, *105*, 106–7, *107*, 108, 120, *121*, 129, 130
  employment in Dubai 125–8
mass flight, and the West-Russia relationship 13
Mearsheimer, John 10, 11
media 15
  and Ukrainian refugees 93–4, 118
Medvedchuk, Viktor 24
mental health issues, Ukrainian refugees 26, 28–9, 117, 119
MIC ('military-industrial complex') 11
  Western military support for Ukraine 24–5
Middle East, migration to Europe from 116
migration, international 16, 115, 116
  mass flight, and the West-Russia relationship 13
  and precarious employment 61–2
  to Spain 32
Milana (research participant) 68, 76, 83, 84, 86, 111, 112, 113, 120
Ministry of Inclusion, Social Security and Migration, Spain 30
Mitchell, B. 12, 61
Moldova, 'Association Trio' 10
moralism 88

Morocco, migrants to Spain 32, 115, 131
multinational corporations 11, 13–14

N

Nastia (Anastasia), (research participant) 37, 40, 41, 42–3, 45–6, 47–8, 53, 54–5, 58–9, 71, 72, 73, 105, *105*, 106–7, *107*, 120
  employment in Estonia 107–8, *121*, 126, 128–31, 130–1
Natasha (research participant) 1–2, 3–4, 6, 8, 15, 16, 22, 23, 26, 32, 34–5, 35–6, 51, 67, 70, 76, 77, 90, 93–4, 134
National Statistics Institute 87
nationalism 115, 116
NATO (North Atlantic Treaty Organization) 12, 115
  enlargement 8, 13
  relationship with Ukraine 8, 9, 10, 24, 25
neoliberalism 1–2, 9, 10–12, 14–15, 17, 19–20, 34, 61, 62, 67, 75, 84, 92, 99, 101, 103, 118, 132
Northrup Grumman 25
nuclear weapons, Russia 11

O

'occupation,' Russian invasion as 23
Oksana (research participant) 37, 40–1, 42–3, 43–4, 45, 46–7, 50, 53, 54, 55–6, 57, 58, 62, 71, 72, 77, 80, 84, 86, 90, 100, *105*, 108–9, 113, 116, *121*, 122, 123–5
Olena (research participant) 35, 51, 64, 72, 73, 77, 96, 97, 103, 104, *105*, 116, 120, *121*
oligarchs, Ukraine 6–7, 8, 12, 24
online translation tools 44, 45
Orange Revolution, 2004/5 7

P

'performative activism' 93
Poland
  Ukrainian migrants to 19
  Ukrainian refugees in 26–7, 96, 120
politics, political torpor 15–16
'poor and needy,' labelling of Ukrainian refugees as 47–8, 63, 79–80, 118
population decline, and the labour market 61
populism 96, 116
Poroshenko, Petro 23–4
positionality, of author 16–19
post-traumatic stress disorder 26, 29, 53
precision-guided munitions 11
privatisation, of social welfare 14
Protection Monitoring Report, Poland 96
protest movements
  in Brunete 71
  'Euromaidan' protests 7–8, 23
  Orange Revolution, 2004/5 7

public spending, impact of neoliberalism on 14
Putin, Vladimir 9, 24, 43, 45

R

Raytheon Technologies 25
Redhead, S. 14–15
refugees
  Ukrainians' rejection of labelling as 47–8, 63
  see also Ukrainian refugees
research
  and ethics 18
  impact of neoliberalism on 17
  informed consent 18–19
Research Laboratory, University of Warsaw 96
Romania 32
  NATO membership 8
Rosa (research participant) 72, 90–1, 92–3
Russia
  annexation of Crimea, 2014 9–10, 16, 23, 24
  BRICS (Brazil, Russia, India, China, South Africa) 13
  invasion of Georgia 9
  and neoliberalism 11
  nuclear weapons 11
  post-Soviet era 6
  propaganda 25, 26
  Ukraine invasion and war, 2022- 2–3, 4, 10, 24–5, 42–3
    failed counteroffensive, 2023 122–3
    impact of and implications for Europe 115–18
    kidnapping of Ukrainian children 123
  Ukraine, relationship with
    geopolitical, structural, cultural and subjective contexts 10–16
    historical overview 5–10
  Ukrainian migrants to 16
  see also Soviet Union
'Russification' of Ukraine 5

S

Sakwa, Richard 9
Sánchez, Pedro 30
Schengen zone 16, 26
Scholz, Olaf 24
Servant of the People 48–50, 78, 119, 123
sexual violence/exploitation risk to Ukrainian refugees 29
Shrooten, M. 28
Simon (research participant) 58, 59, 72, 105, 106, 130
Slava Ukraïni 37
Slovakia, NATO membership 8
Slovenia, NATO membership 8
social media 93

social sciences, impact of neoliberalism on 17
social welfare, impact of neoliberalism on 14
Sofia (research participant) 35, 51, *51*, 77, 86, 95, 96, 97, 98, 99, *105*, *121*
South Asia, migration to Europe from 116
Soviet Union 12
  and Ukraine 1–2, 5–6
  see also Russia
Spain
  employment 32
  housing shortages 27
  labour market 27
  migration to 32
  political, economic and social context 31–4
  precarious employment 61–2
  Ukrainian refugees in 26, 27, 29–31
  see also Brunete, Spain
Spanish Civil War 31
Spanish National Institute of Statistics 61
speed, society's obsession with 15
Stalin, Joseph 5
'Stephania' (Kalush Orchestra) 71–2, 86
Syria 11
  migrants to Europe 28, 36

T

Tanya (research participant) 68, 71, 75, 77, 86, 87, 96, 97, 98, 99–100, *105*, *121*
Temporary Protection Directive, EU (European Union) 26
terrorism, and the West-Russia relationship 13
Thimsen, A.F. 93
Transparency International (TI) 125
'trending causes' 93–4
Turchynov, Oleksandr 7
Tymoshenko, Yulia 8

U

Ukraine
  'Association Trio' 10
  corruption 6–7, 8, 12, 24, 124–5
  culture of
    food culture 44–5
    Servant of the People 48–50
  food production 8
  independence 6, 15–16
  migration 16
  natural energy supplies 8
  neoliberalism 1–2, 11, 12
  oligarchs 6–7, 8, 12, 24
  population loss 16
  relationship with Russia
    geopolitical, structural, cultural and subjective contexts 10–16
    historical overview 5–10
  relationship with the West 7, 13, 24–5
    EU (European Union) 8, 10, 23–4, 25

Index

NATO (North Atlantic Treaty Organization) 8, 9, 10, 24, 25
United Kingdom 24
United States 10, 24–5
Russian invasion and war, 2022- 2–3, 4, 10, 24–5, 42–3
 failed counteroffensive, 2023 122–3
 impact of and implications for Europe 115–18
 kidnapping of Ukrainian children 123
'Russification' of 5
Soviet Union era 1–2, 5–6
Ukrainian refugees 26–7, 116
 in Brunete 2–5, 3, 29–31, 116
  author's experience of hosting 16–17, 40–50
  Brunete Ukrainian Refugee Association 73–4
  bureaucracy and administrative processes 53–6
  childcare issues 68–70, 75, 90, 97–8, 110–11
  cultural integration 4, 53, 70, 78–86, 93, 98, 116, 119–20
  education 53, 54, 57–8, 119
  employment 4, 53, 59–66, 67–8, 101–3, 116, 118–19, 125–8
  experiences of invasion 22–3, 42–3
  hosting and support of 34–7, 64, 65–7, 70, 73–4, 75–94, 95, 96–101, 106, 116–17, 119–20
  protest marches 71
  return to Ukraine 4–5, 88, 95, 108–9, 111, 115, 120–2, 134
  Spanish language learning 53, 70–1, 120, 132–3
 in Canada 26
 in the Czech Republic 26, 27, 46
 in Estonia 107–8, *121*, 126, 128–31, 130–1
 in the EU (European Union) 26, 28
 exodus from Ukraine 25–7
 exploitation/sexual violence risk to 29
 in Germany 26, 27, 104, 120
 hosting 28–36
 and the media 93–4, 118
 mental health issues 26, 28–9, 45–6, 51, 53, 117, 119
 in Poland 26–7, 96, 120
 'poor and needy,' labelling of 47–8, 63, 79–80, 118
 in Spain (generally) 26, 27, 29–31
 in the United States 26
Ukrainian Soviet Socialist Republic *see* Ukraine, Soviet Union era

Ukrainian Territorial Defence Forces 43, 66
Ukrainska Pravda ('Ukrainian Truth') 7
United Kingdom, relationship with Ukraine 24
United Nations
 Russia's annexation of Crimea, 2014 23
United Nations Department of Economic and Social Affairs 16
United Nations High Commission for Refugees 25
United States
 and the collapse of the Soviet Union 12
 Europe's military and security dependence on 116
 MIC ('military-industrial complex') 11
 relationship with Ukraine 10, 24–5
 Ukrainian refugees in 26

V

Valentin (research participant) 1–2, 3–4, 6, 8, 15, 16, 20, 22, 25, 32, 34–5, 35–6, 51, 67, 70, 75–6, 77, 78, 93, 103, 134
Valentyna (research participant) 50–1, *51*, 62–3, 75–6, 77, 78, 82–3, 84–5, 86, 90, *105*, 111, 112, 113, *121*, 121–2
Virilio, Paul 15

W

war crimes 43
Warsaw Pact 9
wealth, concentration of 13–14
Western countries
 neoliberalism and the increase of inequality 14
 relationship with Ukraine 7, 13, 24–5
Winlow, S. 15, 84
Wolff, S. 124

Y

Yana (research participant) 64, 65–6, 100–1, 116, 132–4
Yanukovych, Viktor 7–8, 9, 23
Yemen 11
Yesenia (research participant) 50, *51*, 62, 63, 76, 77, 78, 111, 112, 121, *121*
Yushchenko, Viktor 7–8

Z

Zelenskyy, Volodomyr 24, 124
 Servant of the People role 48–50
Zlata (research participant) 35, 51, *51*, 68, 77, 86, 95, 96, 100, *105*, *121*

www.ingramcontent.com/pod-product-compliance
Lightning Source LLC
Chambersburg PA
CBHW071713020426
42333CB00017B/2257